Discovering
LAZARUS

By
John Kelly

With
Jenny Grace

ISBN 978-1-0980-4438-1 (paperback)
ISBN 978-1-0980-4439-8 (digital)

Christian Faith Publishing, Inc.
832 Park Avenue
Meadville, PA 16335
www.christianfaithpublishing.com

Printed in the United States of America

CONTENTS

PREFACE

I n writing *Finding Lazarus,* I had but one reason in mind. That was to give hope to the hopeless and for all the readers to know that God is the answer. When in doubt, believe and ask for help and have hope. Sitting here writing this preface, I'm thinking about my spiritual rebirth thirty-six years ago. The older you get, the more you realize and embrace your mortality, along with an understanding of the context of time in one's life.

Our life spans are very short compared to eternity. Let's face it—when we die, we're dead forever. Forever is a long time, longer than the world has been in existence. Being a Christian spiritualist and a profound deep thinker, I contemplate a lot about good and evil. I believe there are a lot of good people in this world doing good deeds. These days, I am attuned to being considerate and courteous to my fellow man. I also see those actions as being reciprocal from most people I come across, and most of them are strangers. This gives me hope that this humanism will spread and help mankind to continue to exist and thrive. I look at this as *good energy.*

Then there is my past life, and some of my present professional life as a criminal profiler where I've interacted with murderers and other types of criminals. I was also a criminal at one point in my life until my spiritual awakening and rebirth many years ago. It takes some daring to live the life of the underworld and do things that you know are wrong and hurtful to others, for which I'm extremely sorry, that could land you in prison or worse. I call this *evil energy*.

However, I believe it even takes more daring and courage to turn over control of your life and put your life in God's hands and believe he will direct you and take care of you.

So here we have it: good energy and evil energy. They are both constants in this world. Evil energy is extremely seductive. Take Jesus Christ. From my understanding, he was praying and asking God his Father for help to deliver him from temptation and evil in the Lord's Prayer. This tells us how powerful Jesus felt evil is. If this is the case, knowing that none of us are Christlike, what kind of chance do we have in avoiding temptation and evil alone? We need help! I encourage you to do what Jesus did—reach out. And don't just pray for hope but also have hope and confidence in prayer. I did.

When I look back over my life, I can't even begin to rationalize the evil energy I've seen and been involved in. At times, I am up close and personal with serial killers—the face of pure evil—who have killed many victims and destroyed countless families. This evil energy has caused a mass-murdering trend in our schools and other public places, including churches and synagogues. It has spawned gang growth with new violent members fighting for power and turf control. We see animal abuse growing at epidemic proportions with increased violence. We're witnessing the destruction of the family system in America through horrific child abuse. This evil energy is dripping down onto our children. We also see addictive illness growing into a national health threat nationwide for our families. Yes, the darkness of evil energy is powerful but even more powerful is the light and hope in God. The darkness of night is always vanquished by the light of day.

I called this book *Discovering Lazarus* because not only did I feel that God raised me from a spiritual and physical deadness as he did with Lazarus, but on my way, I also met the renowned Dr. Arnold Lazarus, a great psychologist and theorist. When I asked him to endorse my first book *Warning Signs: A Guidebook for Parents*, he did so gladly. Arnie, whom he liked to be called, helped thousands of people through his books, practice, and teachings. He was also the head of the doctoral program of Psychology at Rutgers University in New Jersey for many years. He was responsible for teaching, training, and turning out thousands of psychologists who would venture into the world and help countless numbers of people suffering from mental illness.

His kindness-filled legacy will live on forever. His humanism didn't stop with his professional practice. Arnie always had several cats whom he had adopted, and some were deaf. He and his wife, Daphne, took care of their cats as if they were their children. Arnie and Daphne were also the type of people who made sure there was something for the garbagemen to eat and drink each week. I am proud to say I learned a lot from being around Arnie. I look to him as a mentor, but more importantly, he became a good and trustworthy friend. I enjoyed staying in contact with him for many years until his death. He made the world a better place, it's humanity's loss.

Interestingly enough, on some days when I left Dr. Lazarus's home in Princeton, I took Route 1 South to Trenton State Prison. This is the home to some of the worst serial killers in New Jersey. There, I met *Thirteen*, a sadistic serial killer. Over the years, I tried to get inside his mind to manipulate him into telling me the names of all the women he killed and where he hid some of their bodies. What a drastic change for me in going from Lazarus, the greatest and kindest humanist I've ever met, to an evil and sadistic serial killer who could care less about his fellow man and only enjoyed torturing and killing women for sexual gratification.

Ten years ago, I authored a quote, "You only know what you know from what you've learned. Who were your teachers?" I put this quote on the face page of our corporate website STALK INC. The meaning I wanted to convey is that we, as human beings, are the sum total of the teachers and that can include everyone and everything we have had along the way and what we have learned. In my case, I broke it down to the good and the evil. For better or for worse, this is who I am now.

In most prefaces, the author gives thanks and names of people who have helped make this book possible, but I could not possibly name all the teachers and experiences that have made me who I am today. So I will just generalize. I want to thank all the wiseguys, sociopaths, psychopaths, murderers, and narcissistic evil-energy criminals whom I've interacted with along the way.

I want to thank all the professionals at Beyond Productions and Investigation Discovery for their great work, producing the show Dark Minds and, especially the Dark Minds on-set team, with whom I was honored to work. You all have brought these cases back to life in the media to one day be solved. You have also given the victims and their families a voice for justice. I commend CBS's 48 hours for it's coverage of these cases, having me on, and trying to help the families find justice, from the very beginning. I also want to thank all the positive, empathetic, and sympathetic friends and professional colleagues who trained me and encouraged me in my journey. You have all taught me well. As for my addicted brothers and sisters, as I mentioned in the beginning, I wrote this book to give hope to the hopeless who may be drowning in despair, depression, and addictive illness. Please continue to have faith in your own journeys. All I can say is if I can do it, so can you.

A grateful Christian recovering addict,

John Kelly

CHAPTER 1

Many, Many Amends

The day I entered St. Francis Cathedral in Metuchen, New Jersey, and made my way to the altar, I believed I had struck rock bottom. The church was empty, and my footsteps on the terrazzo floors echoed against the limestone walls. In the solitude, I found the peace I needed to plead with God. What I prayed for at that moment was for God to take my life out of my own hands, to take my life out of my control, and to run it for me. If this were not possible, sadly, I prayed simply to be allowed to die. In effect, I turned my life over to God.

"I've been negatively using the gifts you gave me—the gift of gab, the gift of manipulation, and the gift of smarts. But if you give me another chance, I will use them in a positive way to help others."

My primary focus was in trying to strike a deal with God. But flashes of the mess I had created kept interrupting my prayers—my frightened wife lying on the floor with sadness and loathing in her eyes of which a man should never cause.

The "For Sale" signs pounded into the soil of our front lawn and the "Space for Rent" fixed to the warehouse door of my business.

"Please help me, and if you do help me, I will make many, many amends. And I'll let you direct my life, and if you won't take my life over and direct it for me, then please take my life from me because I don't know what to do." My best drug-induced delusional thinking brought me to this place.

Through the filter of time through years of healing and a healthy lens, I can now see that this desperate day in the church was not my rock bottom but the beginning of my ascent back from an abyss that I had known for so long. I had forgotten there was hope for any other sort of existence. In this church, which had burned down and was then rebuilt in 1920. I was praying for the guidance I needed, and the simple act of asking was my salvation. I too had been burnt and was in need of rebuilding.

The journey into the abyss began in Pennsylvania and was a slow one, step by step, a process where I lost myself and came to care most about two very convoluted things—money and power. It was not a big stretch of the imagination for my sort of existence to come to be in this small town which was well-known by the Mafia bosses across the country when coal was king. These were insane years filled with clubbing, making deals on and under-the-table, along with discos, and stimulants around the clock—whether in the form of coke or gambling. When you are young and you get a taste of this sort of power and control, you become seduced, and you lose your sense of self and reality it was addicting.

At one time, I also had legitimate businesses, but now they were gone. I had become the perfect stimulant addict, and I inhabited a grandiose world, living for the next high, the next party. The next gamble! The only escape from this concocted world was sleep, but as soon as I awoke, the hustle began all over again—hustling for money and drugs. Earning money was essential to keep it all going, to stay in the game, and continue to enjoy the lifestyle.

A typical day was waking late in the afternoon as the sunlight was already diminishing and regular folks were wrapping up their hours at work. Coffee and a cigarette came first, and then the figuring out how to make a score while I showered before eating a large portion of unhealthy food. At 286 pounds, I was a glutton for food, booze, and for coke. At night, I could put away a fifth of Dewars or two and an eight ball of cocaine, gambling and partying all night only to sleep fitfully. Several times, I nearly overdosed in my sleep. Some nights, I believed I could hear my dead father calling *John* loudly to revive me, which was most definitely psychosis—not the dreams of a young man missing his father who had been dead for many years.

I had been raised by wise guys in the streets who spent their time and energy educating and indoctrinating me to be a young earner with one motivation: for me to make them a lot of money. These wise guys were tough and crazy but definitely not stupid. They knew how to brainwash kids like me into their culture. Their major concern was to be surrounded by people they could trust, even a rare, young Irish kid with reddish blond hair; and I was happy to oblige. I wanted to be accepted. I had proven myself early on the street as a tight-lipped, knock-around guy. Loyalty and trust were necessary for their existence. Since they had access to all the wealth in the world, their major commodity was money.

At fifteen or sixteen, I began to get involved. It was an age where I was most impressed by people who flashed the money, the guys who ran the gambling establishments and had big fancy cars. Some owned bars and poolrooms where dice games, sports betting, horse-race betting, card games, pinball machines with cash prizes, or shooting pool for money were the orders of the day and night. The town was wide open for gambling. The cops were on the arm and turned a blind eye. Gambling was the major industry that kept the town afloat and helped other businesses prosper. This lifestyle was a complete hustle, and the pay certainly beat making two or three dollars—an hour minimum wage in a factory.

But I had not started out this way. I was raised in the Catholic Church and went to a Catholic school for twelve years, and I was focused on wholesome activities like football. I had been a jock, but unfortunately, my school dropped football. And then a drastic change came about. I went from jock to street person, and the street seemed to restore my self-esteem, giving me power as I worked my way up in the underworld of my childhood town.

My hometown was down on its luck. In its day, it had gained prominence on the backs of immigrant coal workers, and there were defined neighborhoods as a result of influx. Over time, dress factories sprang up as a great many manufacturers chose this area of Pennsylvania, knowing they could pay their workers low wages. It lasted as long as it took Chinatown in New York City to introduce slave labor. At this point, the area's apparel factories started to close, leaving no mines and no dress factories! This is where my formative years were spent, where I heard sayings like, "If you go slow, you gotta go. If you go fast, you can't last," "If you can't get along, you gotta get it on," or "Do what you gotta do," and the most catchy one of all: "Cash don't lie."

To a kid, these clichés had weight. They stuck in my head and seemed to make sense. What made even more sense was observing which people had the money, the cars, and the enviable houses in a community that was hard-pressed where employment was scarce. As an impressionable teenage boy, it was not a big stretch to reach the decision that I did—not wanting to be one of the unfortunates who had to struggle for every dollar earned. I had watched the struggle in my neighborhood, living in a modest row house with my grandmother and aunts. When neighbors live on top of one another, there's not a lot left to the imagination. You see the fatigue, the long hours, and the constant worry of the fathers and mothers who are trying to piece together a decent life for themselves and their children.

I did not have the opportunity to see my own mother and father struggle side by side in this little town. My mother was never supposed to have children; she had battled demons no one could see and suffered a breakdown when she believed my father was going off to war. They called it war neurosis. Today I realize it was a form of post-traumatic stress disorder and severe depression. She lost both of her parents as a child, and the only person she had was my father. The thought of losing him to World War II was too much for her to bear. She had a major psychiatric break and went to a mental health institution for four years. My father wasn't drafted but was deferred because he was the only means of support for my mother.

When she left the institution, the drug they tried to settle her with was Thorazine, and despite her breakdown and her medications, my mother begged my father for a child. He could not deny her this one natural wish. My father was told by the doctors at the institution that my mother should not have kids because post-partum depression could trigger another psychotic break.

Approximately two months after my birth, my mother was taken from our house, kicking and screaming while my aunts brought me down to the coal cellar. And she remained hidden from me in an institution for three years. When she finally got out, the family felt it was not safe for me to be around her unsupervised. So I saw her for a long time in supervised visits. It was not until I was eighteen that she was just beginning to recover mentally, but physically, she could not win her battle with pancreatic cancer. She passed away at the age of fifty-five.

My grandmother and aunts tried to fill the parental void in my life, and in doing so, they spoiled me as they brought me up from infancy. Through my childhood years, my father was conspicuously absent—really, I had no relationship with him until he was dying—too late in the game for me. What I was unknowingly searching for, out on the streets in my adolescence, was an older male to nurture me. There was one vital thing I remember my father explaining to me when I was five or six: *you never, ever squeal on anyone.* "If you ever get in trouble, say nothing and call me." Since my father never spent much time with me, this advice really sunk in. In our area, it was a necessity for survival!

I can remember one time when I was around nine or ten years old. I was infatuated with firecrackers cherry bombs and M80s. I finally found a store, and a guy who would sell them to me. I met up with a friend of mine, and we took some cherry bombs and M80s and put them together and made one much larger bomb. We then put this bomb on the side of a building under a rain gutter in an alley and lit the fuse. The bomb went off, creating a deafening sound and blowing part of the building off along with the rain gutter. All the neighbors came running, and somebody called the cops. When the cop showed up, he grabbed my friend, who in a fit of tears, ratted me out. The cop then found and grabbed me and asked me where I got the cherry bombs and M80s. I told him I found them! At that point, my aunts, who came running as well to see what happened, went crazy and started to beat and kick me to the ground.

"Johnny, tell the policeman where you got them!"

"I found them!" I said.

They took me home and called my father. He said I did a good thing by not squealing, went to the police station, and made my restitution by saying he would pay for the damages to the building.

To be honest, I didn't see much of him after that. With a missing father figure, the wise guys and the other kids I hustled with became my adoptive family. My best friend Bobby and I came up together. We felt we were connected, that we belonged, and most importantly, we were becoming someone. In reality, these wise guys were making the money. They were molding us into earners and making us believe we were family. For me, it was an illusion. We really were just kids searching for a family. However, family love was not what I found and is not what led me to beg and bargain with God at the age of thirty-two after years of abusing myself and those I loved.

What led me to New Jersey and to St. Francis Cathedral was a demented and twisted journey. At the age of twenty-one, I moved away from the row houses and the neighborhood I had known all my life. I had arrived, purchasing my own house from a bookmaker—an owner of a poolroom and a guy I worked for and respected. This house was nice, spacious with an apartment upstairs, a big piece of property, a two-car garage, and a carport. I was single and a homeowner and moving fast into the world of gambling and its culture as well as into the world of drugs. I also had legitimate jobs by day, selling appliances and plumbing supplies. I got married to my childhood sweetheart who I had been with since we were fifteen years old. The marriage was good for about six years until my addictions progressed. For about three years after that, I lived like a creature of the night—a vampire, so to speak—sleeping all day, out all night, and running my own warehouse business into the ground. Cocaine became my sustenance, and my entire world was cracking beneath my unsteady feet—a huge cocaine habit accompanied by a fifth of Scotch daily. I ran a tab at the bar and bought drinks and gave away coke that amounted to probably hundreds of dollars per night.

While you are in it, you cannot see, and I had no idea when the undeniably ugly end to all this came crashing down upon my head. Two nights back to back revealed my unraveling. The first was a dark night in a hotel with an eight ball of blow, a fifth of Dewars, and a gun my only company. The party was truly over. There were no more friends; I was crazy, broke, and alone. I tried to conjure up the rush of the nightlife and of the power I thought I could always count on, but that was impossible to do in the stone-cold silence. No more big crowds surrounding me as I placed hundred dollar bills down on the gleaming bar or gave away coke like it was penny store candy. No more hearing my name called "Mr. Kelly" pumping my ego as we were escorted past the snaking club line and into a private room where we could do whatever we desired. As long as I was buying, the leeches held on. I was addicted to it all—not just the drugs and the booze but the power of being in the life and loving it.

This night in the hotel, I was wasted out of my mind; paranoia had sunk its tentacles into the nooks and crannies of my head as it had done before. I looked out of the window and across the way. And even through the blackness surrounding the hotel, I could make out a guy on the rooftop, clutching a glinting rifle, trying to get a bead on me. I gathered up my booze and my coke and ran into the bathroom, shutting off the lights, so he couldn't see my movements. But the hours were ticking by, and he was still out there waiting. I sat in the bathroom shaking, snorting, and drinking, holed up in there knowing I was a dead man if I dared to emerge. *I'll just wait him out 'til daylight* was all I could summon up as a logical thought. I was in there for hours.

In the morning, the phantom shooter was gone, but my paranoia and psychosis remained close by—two companions I could still rely upon when the others had vanished into the nightclub vapor. This was not the first time my insanity had grabbed ahold of me. I truly believed there were people out there who intended on doing me some harm. How I never shot anyone or got shot, I'll never know. In those days, I carried a weapon as casually as carrying a cell phone.

The following night was the turning point enhanced by my insanity from cocaine-induced psychosis. My wife, the love of my life, and I got into a heated argument, and I threw her down, kicked her in the back, and then contemplated suicide. I was filled with crazy despair and sat clutching a gun until sunlight came pouring through the windows and lit up the living room and kitchen. This sunlight somehow brought me to my senses. I threw down the gun and went to bed. When I awoke, my wife was gone. She did not return, and though I did not realize it at the time, her courageous act saved my life along with starting me on a path, to not only help myself, but to help thousands of others along the way. It's a sobering thing to lose your wife, your business, and your home. This was my bottom.

During my drive from Pennsylvania to Edison, New Jersey, where I was to live with my aunt while fighting my way into recovery, a song by The Who came over the radio—"Behind Blue Eyes." The lyrics resonated as the highway miles slipped beneath the wheels of my car, which was soon to be repossessed.

"No one knows what it's like to be the bad man, to be the sad man…" even though my eyes are green not blue and "my dreams they aren't as empty as my conscience seems to be." These lyrics sank into my heart as I gripped the steering wheel, flashing back to the *For Sale* sign on my home to the television I had to sell that morning for 150 bucks just to have some pocket money, and to my closed business, the empty warehouse.

I recalled being alone in the empty warehouse one night, peering outside into the falling rain as I stood in the garage doorway, believing there was no way out. I was certain I was to continue on this path to self-destruction—I would continue with the drugs until I killed myself. There was a complete sense of hopelessness and worthlessness as I saw the only escape was to party my way out of this life. I was a junkie! Someone I would have bet my life on I would never have become. We always said, "Do the drugs. Don't let the drugs do you." But the drugs had done me! The deep feelings of depression and despair gazing out into darkness of evening and rain returned and most of all, the incident of attacking my frightened wife plagued me. Only by the grace of God had I not fired that gun. This had been the worst day of my life. I had been raised never to strike a woman. This is how insane I was; this is what drugs will do to you. What sort of monster had I turned into?

That morning, the last person I saw before leaving my hometown was Vinny, a friend and a hardcore dealer, who was bitten by his own snake. He was quite a character and pretty crazy. He would spotlight deer off-season, drive around the mountain, hit the stunned deer with his headlights, blow it away, throw the corpse in the trunk of his Cadillac, and bring it home, skin it, and keep the meat. This guy was strung out himself and trying to keep his family afloat. When he heard I was leaving, Vinny asked me to meet him on my way out. I parked my car in the shade and walked across the grass toward my friend and his tiny daughter who was trying to learn how to pump her legs on the swing. I smiled—all the while having a flashback of sitting around their dining room table and snorting coke with Vinny and his wife and a couple of other guys all night long. The house was in complete disarray as if there had been months of partying, and no one had bothered to clean up. Dirty dishes and sticky floors, but none of that stopped us from doing our coke or thing.

For some reason, on that last day, seeing Vinny with a pistol tucked into his belt, reality hit me: this is a bad, bad situation. This man is going down the tubes too. He said, "You've got to understand something. When you're straight and clear and this is all behind you, realize I don't have your money. I have my own problems, my own habit, and I only have a few thousand dollars to my name. But I don't want you mad at me." He gave me a bump for the road. I pointed my car toward Jersey, and I left.

Little did I know that two months later, Vinny would walk into an Italian social club and get a beating from a martial artist after an argument ensued at the bar. Then Vinny would dust himself off, go home, get one of his pistols, and come back to the club to shoot the guy in front of everybody—but not kill him. This guy was extremely lucky! Vinny didn't play! He did some time, and when he got out and was still on probation or parole, he got caught up one night in a high-speed chase with the cops. He must have had drugs or guns in his car. He ended up crashing and dying as he tried to get away from the police.

I had made out better than Vinny would, pleading with God for my salvation in St. Francis Cathedral. What I didn't know yet was if God would answer my prayers. In my mind, I didn't believe he would let alone that he would empower me to take an unbelievable journey.

CHAPTER 2

New Beginnings

The further Pennsylvania became in my rear view mirror, the more miraculous it seemed that I survived. *Why me?* I often wondered. *Why did I survive?* When I landed at my aunt's house in Edison, New Jersey, a sedate suburban area that may as well been another planet, I found myself physically ill. Bleeding ulcers had resulted from the insane amount of booze I had been drinking, causing me to spit up blood. Blood streamed from my nose due to the copious supply of coke I had been snorting, and blood was there to greet me in the porcelain toilet each day from the booze. I was a mess—a complete mess some 80 pounds overweight at about 286 pounds with a forty-six- to forty-eight-inch waist that kept me from clothes shopping in a regular store. I had to go to the Big Men's store just to get a pair of pants to go around my waist.

Things weren't any better mentally. I couldn't focus on reading—even the simplest sentences on a page were a challenge, and my memory, forget about it! Truth be told, I was not employable. In my hometown, we hadn't needed to read books. We hadn't needed a lofty vocabulary or academic intellect. All we needed to maneuver were street smarts. Life in Pennsylvania had been incredibly cut and dry.

Soon, I realized my memory was shot too as I attempted to read a book that dealt with brain chemical, depleted neurotransmitters. How was a strung-out guy from a coal-mining town going to redeem himself? I think one of the worst problems an addict has trying to attempt recovery is realizing he has a conscience. The further you get away from the substance and into recovery, the bigger your conscience grows, if you have one and the guiltier you feel. I think the lyrics in the Goo Goo Dolls' song "Iris" are appropriate here. "And I don't want the world to see me 'cause I don't think they'd understand. When everything's made to be broken, I just want you to know who I am."

The problem is that the addict knows how to medicate his guilt and bury it. Relapse will do the trick! Unfortunately, I found out that when you bury feelings, you bury them alive. And sooner or later, no matter how many years, they will come back to haunt you. I strove to overhaul my day-to-day existence, waking up in the morning and heading outside for walks that eventually turned into runs and weight lifting. I remember running to "Angry Young Man," a song by Styx:

"Get up, get back on your feet. You're the one they can't beat and you know it."

I lost a total of eighty-four pounds in eighteen months. I was reading in my down time to learn about vitamins and nutrients to rebuild my brain and replace neurotransmitters, spending my hours after work meditating and praying—basically exercising both my body and my mind daily in ways I had never imagined let alone done.

This was no easy process. The nightmares, night terrors, and cold sweats continued as did the disturbing and traumatic flashbacks. It was impossible to forget having the barrel of a gun placed to my head, a knife stuck into my neck, or bloody bar fights when your life is genuinely threatened and you're at risk of being killed—you don't conveniently forget.

Somehow, I found full-time employment, working at an appliance store in the warehouse in the morning and then at an appliance store showroom in the afternoon. These jobs were a challenge. The warehouse was hot in the summer, freezing in the winter, and demanded a great deal from me physically. Conversely, the appliance store tapped my cognitive abilities and made me all too aware of my ADD. My aunt witnessed my struggles and prompted me to get some counseling—especially for my addiction. I found a young female social worker who was still interning in a clinic mostly filled with heroin addicts, and she helped me through my first phases of therapy and recovery. This therapist convinced me that I was worth saving. This was the beginning of the cocaine epidemic of the 1980s, and there was not much available in the way of treatment. Here I was just beginning my own journey of recovery with my brain and body shot, but my grandiose entrepreneurial spirit reared up as I imagined a center in the mountains of Pennsylvania to help coke addicts.

The reality was that my recovery was still in its infancy, and I was terrified of slipping back into my old ways. This fear produced a healthy strategy: staying home. I could not risk being around bars or any other scene where I could score some coke. If I slipped again, it would be the end. Once your brain is addicted to coke depending on how much you're using, it takes many years to desensitize yourself. Even watching movies or news shows that alluded to coke seemed risky. So it was work or home, church or home, and the gym or home. I had no idea that it would take five grueling years to beat this insidious drug hunger.

After a solid year of recovery (and I give a lot of credit to Narcotics Anonymous and counseling), my uncle somehow talked me into going to Bennigan's, a nearby pub and restaurant. Even though twelve months had passed, I was still a broken person both mentally and physically. I had dropped about forty pounds, and my exercise and nutrition were restoring me physically. But there was a common saying in AA and NA that it takes five years to get your brains back, and I didn't have five years to wait. I had to get my neurotransmitters back ASAP. I had already lost everything—my business, my house, my wife, and nearly, my own life. I was haunted by major sleep disorders: PTSD, flashbacks, and alarming memory deficits. And it was at this low point in my life in a Menlo Park Bennigan's that I met Marilyn, a beautiful and intelligent woman in her late twenties.

Though we hit it off right away, I believed we were simply two ships passing in the night. She was honest to a fault and spoke openly about her rare and progressive autoimmune disease for which there was no cure—Takayasu's arteritis—also known as *pulseless disease*. But despite her poor health caused by her own body's immune system constricting her arteries, Marilyn cared for herself, taking walks and paying careful attention to her health. Strange to imagine that two young people fighting for our lives had found one another, but our common ground was not enough. Marilyn recognized the tough road ahead of me as an addict in recovery and decided this was not the relationship for her.

Nearly a year later, my aunt was dying from cancer, and she ended up in the hospital where Marilyn worked. We were fated to cross paths again. I had continued working on my recovery since we'd met, attending NA meetings, going to church, meditating, and slowly clawing my way back to sanity. At this point, my weight was down to 202 pounds. I was more fit from running, lifting weight and taking care of my nutrition, and Marilyn agreed to go out with me. Maybe she could see for herself that I was committed to my full recovery. There was no mistaking it. We became a loving team, taking walks together, lending one another emotional support, and trying to get on our feet financially.

Then one day, a phone call came from Steven Altman, an extremely well-known criminal attorney in New Brunswick. Steve was a senior partner of Benedict and Altman. He was extremely well-dressed and well-spoken. Most importantly, to me, he was a good man and a stand-up guy. Steve was an upfront lawyer—there was no bullshit with him. His partner, Joe Benedict, was the same way. These two guys were a pair of prosecutors back in the day who paid their dues and were now great defense attorneys. They were known to other criminal defense attorneys in Jersey, as Marris and Mantle, for all the cases they won. Their clients came first, not the money.

Apparently, the FBI wanted to talk to me. My Pennsylvania days were hard to shake. Steven had represented me some years back on an interstate gambling charge when I got busted, laying off action to a faction of the Gambino family. He got me off with three years' probation, and wouldn't you know with my luck, the probation officer tried to get me to take his car over to New York and burn it for the insurance money? Can you imagine? This was a man who was supposed to help rehabilitate me.

To make a long story short, I didn't rat him out either, but I had a good up close and personal talk with him. He moved me to another probation officer and sometime later he was arrested. It seems I was not the only person he was extorting. Steve was brilliant and truly concerned and committed to his clients. Even though I trusted in his professional skills, meeting with the FBI, when my mental abilities were still not fully functioning, was not a great prospect.

In our meeting, the FBI laid out what they wanted in no uncertain terms—reminding me that I was nothing but a busted-out junkie who was pretty much done. They told me that my friends back in Pennsylvania might not just let me walk around in light of what I knew. It could be just a matter of time before they put out a contract on me if they hadn't already. The agents wanted me to inform on a close friend of mine, my best friend Bobby; and they suggested that I come up with a sum of money that they'd give me to go do whatever I wanted. As I stared at these two agents from across the table, I said they'd probably be doing me a favor if they killed me.

Bobby had done what is known as *putting me on the shelf.* I had owed quite a few people money after I ran bad from drugs, and he had given me the pass I needed, covering some of my debts and providing me the opportunity to leave for New Jersey and attempt my recovery from cocaine. I let the agents know there was no way I would inform on my friend, to which they responded I was being brought up before a grand jury, and if I were indicted, they would put me away for a long time. I still insisted I didn't have any information for them.

Steve Altman told them, "That's it, guys." And I sat back uneasily and waited to see if I would be indicted. I had not forgotten the lesson my father had instilled in me as a child. One thing I felt down to my core: There was no way anyone I knew would ever serve a single day due to my testimony. I'm no rat, and no one ever did.

Whether it was incredible luck to have Bobby and Steven looking out for me or whether God was working overtime, these two men coming to my rescue was truly good fortune. Little did any of us know at the time that because they helped me, thousands of people would be saved from drug addiction. Steven was not only a fantastic lawyer, but he was also a true humanist. He represented me for free because he knew I was broke and down on my luck. His friendship and unbelievable help would continue faithfully throughout the years. At that time, I never realized I would have the honor of working as an expert side by side with him and the other great attorneys at Benedict and Altman. Because of them, many addicts were sent to the correct rehabilitation treatment and saved.

It's impossible not to glance back and remember myself as a little boy walking into a Catholic Church with my Bible in hand and then to recount every gruesome thing I'd been through to somehow end up back in the arms of God. I truly believe if you are willing to turn it all over, to pray, or to meditate to God or Jesus or whatever higher power you believe in, only good will come. It doesn't cost anything to ask God for help, which is exactly what I did during the FBI crisis.

After informing Marilyn I might have to go away for a while, I chose a quiet afternoon to pray in St. Francis Church. The wooden pews were empty, and nothing but serenity surrounded me. I prayed to God to watch over me and for his will to be done if I were to be federally indicted. It was so quiet you could have heard a pin drop with its infinitesimal sound reverberating up to the rafters. Somehow in the silence of my prayers and the peace of this church, I heard an older man's voice utter "Rest in peace." Just three simple words. I was not hallucinating. I hadn't done coke in over a year and a half. There was no mistaking that I heard this voice. Who knows where it came from? Of course I've asked myself this question for over thirty-four years now. Was it someone playing some kind of prank, or was it the real deal? The bottom line is that I was meant to hear those three words at that precise time in that church.

Miraculously, in the end, I was never indicted by the FBI. Maybe they were just bluffing. Somehow, I never faced any legal charges. About a year later, while working at the appliance store, I felt a lump in my neck. I was seen by an ear, nose, and throat specialist through my HMO. After evaluating me, he said he wasn't sure what it was, and he wanted me to be admitted to the hospital for a biopsy at Robert Wood Johnson Hospital. I was placed in a semiprivate room on the cancer unit. *Whoa!* I thought, *This is not a very good situation. Everyone is on chemo.*

For the next few days, I had a number of doctors examining me and asking the same questions over and over: "Have you been out of the country?" "Have you been bitten by any bugs?" "Does cancer run in your family?"

My roommate at the time was a multimillionaire who was dying from stomach cancer. As I would walk out of the room and sneak down the stairwell for a smoke, I had the realization that here I was, a bust-out drug addict in recovery, trying to get back on his feet, lying next to a well-known and respected man—a man who is affluent and has helped many people—and now he's dying. How ironic! I grew up my whole life being obsessed with and chasing wealth, and what does it all mean in the end? This was another spiritual awakening for me. I learned that you can take your spirituality into the grave with you but not your wealth—or anything else for that matter. At that point, what's more important anyway? The biopsy was taken, and it came back negative for cancer. They said it was an infection of some sort and put me on antibiotics.

I simply went on with my recovery, building a life with Marilyn by my side. Our path was not an easy one. We were living in Marilyn's apartment in a house nestled in a bad section of Perth Amboy. After two years, the owner of the house wanted us out, so she could rent it to her granddaughter. Our credit rating and income were not sound enough to secure an apartment in a complex. She had a job as an assistant in human resources at JFK Medical Center in Edison, and she was working her way up in management. Keep in mind: we didn't have any place to live.

Well, again, there was some inexplicable higher power at work. We just met this superintendent at one apartment complex and explained we were looking to rent. He said to come on over and meet his wife. And we just hit it off with them. We filled out an application for the apartment and were told "Absolutely no problem." They just said to come on in. They never even checked the application. If they had checked the application, there's just no way he'd have rented us the apartment. My credit was bad—the repossessed house and my car and my truck. So again, it was like we were led every step of the way with someone watching over us.

As we worked tirelessly to save and better ourselves, we also worked on our relationship. Before we were even married, Marilyn came to believe that I was fighting depression and anger, and she insisted on my returning to therapy. She found a psychologist in Edison who had a good reputation. I made an appointment with him, and Marilyn and I would go together to talk to him about my issues. She arrived at my aunt's house to pick me up, just as my drunken uncle and I were getting into a fight. He had disrespected my aunt, and I lost it. Marilyn arrived to witness me beating and kicking my uncle. I guess I was going to the right place! My therapeutic journey was an interesting one to say the least, and I was soon put on antidepressants for a time to help deal with my depression and moods while I continued to gain ground.

Somehow, despite our financial shortcomings, we managed to save money and build up our credit. I started to do volunteer work with adolescents who were abusing substance at Raritan Bay Medical Center, an inner city hospital in Perth Amboy, New Jersey. While there, I pursued my education to become a certified addiction specialist and social worker. This was an arduous program with a three-year internship—forty hours a week, fifty weeks out of the year, 280 hours of course work, and 6000 hours of on-the-job-training. This was the best thing professionally that could have happened to me. I had the opportunity to work under doctors, really solid professionals, who taught me an awful lot from the other side of the equation.

In March of 1986, I was hired by Dennis Mannsman, a great mentor and teacher at the Youth Co-op across the street from the medical center in the outpatient program. I believe if it were not for Dennis Mansmann, who was God sent, I would never have had the opportunity to continue on my journey. At this point, I was in recovery more than four years. When I reflect upon this time in my life with Marilyn, it's just impossible not to recognize the divine intervention at work. The minister who married us at the Episcopal Church, Father Rodney Cruise, ended up introducing me to Dennis Mansmann, a priest who had been the head vicar in Jamaica. How all these pieces fell into place is astounding. Father Rodney Cruise, who was the pastor of St. Peter's Episcopal Church in Perth Amboy, referring me to Dennis Mansmann, who was the executive director of the Addiction Department at Raritan Bay, was truly a gift. I was only hired for about $7.50 an hour. At this point, I stopped doing volunteer work and went to work full-time. They sent me back to school, paid for my schooling, and helped me not only to get my certification but also to become board certified in addiction and social work.

Crazy things went on in this clinic that I managed to skirt, and eventually, I was promoted by Dennis and thankfully moved to an inpatient program in the hospital, a half-psych, half-addiction floor. This was a place where you got to see it all—withdrawal, mental health, and complicated addictions. I was faced to face with the inner city of Perth Amboy for nearly five years, and I was able to draw upon my own recovery experiences—if I could do this and if I could accomplish what I accomplished, then they could do it too. This is also the place where I got to be supervised and trained by Dr. James O'Connell. He was a true professional and a great supervisor. He was excellent in cognitive and behavioral therapy and exceled in supervision. He really cared about his patients, and there were many sick and complicated patients here who got well because of Jim. The training I received from him was invaluable to my career.

I truly believed and still do that I'm not special. I also truly believed and still do that we can come out of our physical and emotional hell if we want to put an effort into our recovery, but we have to want to do it. It's a self-help situation that no one but the person himself can tackle. Even though God may be watching over all of us, I believe we have to assert ourselves and ask God for help and turn ourselves over to his will. That's when recovery can take place. I've seen it with many other addicts who were really destitute. I've seen the miracles of recovery. I've seen the miracles in the rooms of Alcoholics and Narcotics Anonymous. I've seen the miracles in churches. I've seen people who've had eighty detoxes, a hundred detoxes, or twenty rehabs who have been written off that they'll never get better because "once a junkie, always a junkie." That's not true. I've seen all of that turn around. I've seen people change, and the one thing they all seem to have in common: they have a spiritual program. They have a higher power. They have God in their lives.

What has always resonated the most for me is helping people believe in themselves and motivating them. There is no place for belittling. They do enough of that to themselves but only room to empower them with positive feedback for things well done in recovery. It's also important to set consequences if they can't do recovery in an outpatient basis and to encourage them to go for longer more intensive inpatient care.

All of these experiences and beliefs formed the foundation of my career and formed the core of my practice. One of the most daunting problems for addicts is that they are their greatest critics. The more they pay attention to the critic inside their head, the more stressed and/or depressed they're going to become—and the more likely they're going to seek drugs or some other kind of feel-good experience to take them out of their heads and keep them from physical withdrawal. Most of the time, the belief system of an addict is really messed up. If you are filled only with negative thoughts and these thoughts create negative feelings, why wouldn't you want to look for something to take you away from feeling so bad?

In evaluating a client, one question I would ask is, "Why do you do drugs?"

The usual answer would be "to get high."

I would then say, "What does getting high mean to you?"

The vast majority of the time, they would answer, "To feel good."

I would follow that up with "Why don't you feel good without drugs?"

The way they answered this question unveiled some of the main issues that had to be dealt with in my treatment approach.

I studied my books. I studied the addicts who came through the door. I studied what other doctors and social workers were doing. And all of this knowledge became the effective tool in helping me help others. The most important thing when you're counseling is rapport, and the quickest way to gain rapport is to have something in common. So when a client was sitting across from me, I could see myself some years ago in his situation. When a client would state that he was feeling like he couldn't see the light at the end of the tunnel, I would share a little about my addiction. I would share how my addiction took away my first wife, my house, and my businesses. I would share how I lost everything and became homeless until my aunt gave me a room in her home. Sharing this story seemed to give them hope. "If I can do it, you can do it" was my mantra to them. All you need to do (and I know it sounds easy, but it's not) is to "take it one day at a time."

Every addict wants it right away. They're used to getting their drug, getting high, and getting that instant gratification. Recovery is a one-day-at-a-time process. You never know what's going to be sent your way. So by sharing my story of what I had gone through and how I survived, it helped a lot of people.

To be able to make a career from all of this—well, I couldn't ask for anything better than to make a living while also getting the gratification of helping others. You can't walk the walk for anyone else. But you can be a guide, and you can do the reframing. You can help a person see different ways to deal with things. You can show them a path to walk. It's up to them if they'll walk it or not, but when they stumble, you can be there to help with ideas about what can be done and to provide them with some tools to help him navigate the trek. So you know, the whole thing is very spiritual. I'm very fortunate. In fact, I'm blessed.

In the end, why had I survived was no longer the question. I had a clear understanding that my purpose was to help other addicts and to shed some much-needed light on addictions of all kinds. My true work had really only just begun.

CHAPTER 3

ExtraCare and STALK

In 1991, I opened the doors of ExtraCare Health Services in Old Bridge, New Jersey. A small one room office. Marilyn and I had a great deal of faith and an equal amount of drive. Although we only had $450 to spare, it was our strong faith that provided the seed for what would become one of the most successful counseling centers in the state. My philosophy was rooted in an individualized program, one in which the treatment was created around the client.

At this time, treatment programs were focused around group therapy based upon the twelve-step program which ran just fine with a low budget—one clinician with a group of eight to twelve people. But when you stop and think about it, doctors don't treat every single diabetic the same way. After all, we don't share the same DNA, and we need medical care that is individually tailored. Addictive illness is no different, and group therapy does not work for everyone. I believe firmly that training in various therapies is essential—some respond to cognitive therapy, others behavioral therapy, psychodynamic therapy, reality therapy, twelve-step therapy, or Christian therapy. As a therapist, you have to be an authentic chameleon to establish a rapport and trust. This was the foundation of our center along with a strong focus on building self-esteem, so our clients could regain control of their lives.

Obviously, my own unique experiences with addiction and recovery had a powerful influence on ExtraCare's foundation. The tools I had at my fingertips were the Twelve-Step Program and cognitive therapy. I tried to help my clients get rid of self-defeating thoughts and to embrace being positive. Every addict feels low. Once you cross that line and go from abuse into addiction, your pride may keep you from showing it, but underneath that addiction, you feel horrible about yourself. The only way to escape the reality of the thought that you've messed up your life is to continue using. The guiltier you feel, the more you use; and the more you use, the guiltier you feel. It's a self-perpetuating cycle that continues like a merry-go-round that you can't get off. Like a merry-go-round from hell.

In the beginning phase of opening our center, we could not even afford an office phone. We used the phone in our apartment, and that got pretty crazy because we'd be getting calls all hours of the evening and early in the morning. I brought the success I'd had working with a lot of clients at the hospital in individual and group therapy. It was a word-of-mouth following, but it took a while before I could hire other counselors. Maybe a year and a half, two years before I could hire my first great counselor, Roger, who was from the hospital. Any decent program needs a good family therapist, so about six months later, I brought on an extremely committed and talented female therapist, Lindy, whom I had also known very well from the hospital; she handled the families. Most of our clientele were male. There were some females, but it was like a nine-to-one ratio back in those days. We brought on another female therapist to handle primary care.

We had a small group, and everything was focused on the client as well as the client's family. We might counsel people for a few hours a week, but their families were with them a lot more, and they had more of an idea of what was going on. It's odd. Even to this day, you don't have that much focus on the family. Programs throw twenty various family members together in a room to educate, but when the person gets out of treatment, there isn't that connection. There should be a focus. Let's work through some of these issues that you have with your family because a lot of addicts truly have issues with their families. Likewise, the family has issues with them; and rightfully so, and you need to clear the air to get a fresh start.

There was such passion in my heart motivating me to help guide these addicts, as well as their families, day after trying day. It's important to recognize that the whole family is affected, and their involvement is vital. Anger is often at the root of addictive illness. The question is: who is the anger toward? What's the anger about?

Usually, this destructive emotion is family-centered. Something in the family's system, like incessant criticism before or after enabling the addict's behavior, has caused the addict to internalize his or her anger, medicate the anger, and keep it submerged with drugs or booze. So the more the family is educated on the clients issues, the better off everyone will be. The addict plays a role in the family, sometimes the hero, the mascot, the scape goat, or the forgotten child. It's very important to identify the addict's role and bring this role to the family's attention, so they understand. If he or she gets into recovery and there is no clear understanding, healing can be consciously or unconsciously sabotaged, and the addict can be relegated back into the same destructive role. Any system resents change, and it is challenging for families to relinquish the roles they've so carefully constructed. The treatment approach I put into place at the center was to stabilize the addict, and at the same time, work on the issues whether they be personal or within the family.

Despite the focus on family, whatever our clients said in their sessions was completely confidential—unless they were going to hurt themselves or somebody else. The focus of the therapy had to be on their realizing as human beings. Their birthright is that they deserve love, respect, and value; and they had to learn how to treat themselves in this way and stop the self-destructive behavior.

The success of ExtraCare was undeniable and brought me tremendous gratification. I would like to thank all the clients that I was privileged to serve at ExtraCare counseling centers for over twenty-five years. In no time, ExtraCare grew into three centers in three different counties with nine devoted therapists: a licensed clinical psychologist, licensed certified and master's level social workers, licensed and certified drug and alcohol counselors, consulting psychiatrists, certified addiction specialists, and a pastoral counselor.

My treatment plan flew in the face of the clinical approach of the time, as well as in the face of the addiction field. Soon, our center became one of the primary treatment centers for ATT, Ford, Merck, Lucent, and GM; we were selected by some of the big companies, and again, simply by word of mouth.

It became all too clear that most addicted clients who came in for treatment had underlying issues due to trauma—physical abuse, sexual abuse, or emotional abuse there was also a lot of underlying anxiety and depression. When something lurks underneath—low self-esteem or low self-worth—a great deal of distress ensues, and then the addictive illness leads to self-medication. Of course the more medication needed, the more the reliance on the substance of choice, and then eventually, there's a monumental problem: the issues are still there as well as the physical dependency on the drugs.

In 1992, Marilyn and I tried to keep a healthy balance in our lives. We decided on taking a Canadian vacation, and I brought along a nonfiction book about a serial killer *The Final Payoff* by Ian Mulgrew, which I read on the train as we traveled north. The subject of this book, Clifford Olson, had come from an alcoholic family—similar to the ones we helped at ExtraCare.

This similarity started me thinking along a fresh trajectory, so when we returned from vacation, I began extensive research on other serial killers: what sort of families they had grown up in and whether or not there was alcohol, drug abuse, or physical abuse.

Interestingly, having a conscience is something you learn, and if you are raised in a family that shows you no love or concern, if you are shown no empathy or feelings but only neglect and abuse, how can you have empathy or feelings for others?

In 1993, after spending a great deal of time delving into this subject and researching every possible nook and cranny, I published an article "The Alcohol, Drugs & Serial Killer Connection." I wrote:

> How responsible are alcohol, abuse and other drugs in the serial killers' family backgrounds and personal lives for their depicted murderous behaviors? Would Manson, Lucas, Gary, Gacy, Bundy and Dahmer have killed anyway? No one knows. However, the known facts are that alcohol and other drugs can be powerful uninhibitors that can release and compound feelings of anger and rage, along with sexual urges. These feelings would normally be controlled in sobriety. Alcoholic and drug addicted families perpetuate many serious forms of abuse.

The reason this analysis is so essential comes down to one simple word—*prevention*. Since many serial killers are alcoholics and other chemical abusers before they begin killing, early detection and intervention is key. I wrote:

> As counselors, we are in a position to recognize and intervene (through a Mental Health referral) on a person who has the potential to be a serial killer. This is especially true for those counselors who work primarily with adolescents. By adding some questions to our assessments, we may recognize clients with a potential for progressive violence.
>
> Some questions to be added to an assessment are:
>
> 1. Is client violent toward others? Many serial killers express violence early on toward others, usually younger siblings or younger children.
> 2. Is there a history of illegal or antisocial acts? Most serial killers broke the law frequently as adolescents.
> 3. Has the client displayed unusual cruelty toward animals? Most serial killers have tortured and killed animals as children.

4. Does the client exhibit feelings of guilt or remorse? Most sociopaths will not exhibit these feelings.

5. Is there a background of arsonist tendencies? Fire starting could be an early sign of sociopathic dangerousness.

6. Is there a demonstration of hyper-sexuality? Many serial killers are constantly fantasizing about sex and violence as adolescents.

7. Has client been sexually or physically abused as a child? Most serial killers have experienced one or both types of abuse, and may have sustained traumatic head injuries.

These days, we believe substance abuse is a major precursor for child abuse. And child abuse is the major precursor for serial killers, which is frightening, considering our epidemic of addiction and substance abuse. Thankfully, not everybody who is abused will become a serial killer, but it seems every serial killer was abused. This knowledge initiated my research and led to my putting together an addictions' profile to enhance the FBI and other behavioral and psychological profiles in an attempt to apprehend various serial killers. In effect, I entered the world of serial killing, perceiving it as an addiction. Ultimately, I longed to interview these serial killers face-to-face in an attempt to flesh out and strengthen my theories.

In 1994 or 1995, all of this study and focus led to the formation of System to Apprehend Lethal Killers (STALK) Inc. At this time, I would like to express my heartfelt sympathies and condolences to the victims and their families of such murderous evil.

This was no easy task because there was no money for our organization. The seed money ended up coming from Marilyn and me, and we couldn't pay anyone. So we searched for talent, and five people signed on to help the general public catch serial killers without making a dime for fourteen years. They simply worked pro bono.

This was a well-rounded profiling team of professionals whose mission was to aid law enforcement in the apprehension of serial killers through a comprehensive profiling process. The people I ended up recruiting were well-versed in the psychological, behavioral, and addiction fields. Along with our homicide detectives, this added up to a team second to none and was comprised of Frank Adamson, the Frank Adamson, retired Chief of detectives and commander who ran the Green River Case, Tom Zalesky, law enforcement liaison; Ruth Moore, a nurse specialist of childhood trauma; John Lukiewitz, sexual addiction specialist; and Dr. Mersky in the field of psychology.

Many believe there is a sociopathic gene to blame for becoming a serial killer, but there is research that shows some who supposedly have the genetic predisposition who are raised in good, caring, and loving homes never go on to kill or hurt anybody at all. So our team had to consider whether we were looking at a gene or at an underlying trauma from physical, sexual, or emotional abuse—or both. Just about every single serial killer, I researched or talked to in person had been extremely and severely abused as a child. We began putting our profiles together, and we made certain we covered all the bases. Focusing on a serial killer addiction was one of the most important dynamics for me. Just like any other addict, serial killers are all different, and everyone has a unique ritual just as every addict does not use in the same way. So when STALK put together our profiles, we attempted to individualize and boil them down to the nth degree to get an idea of the killer's personality and behavior.

We determined that serial killers are primarily auditory and visually-oriented, which has a tremendous influence on the type of predator for whom we were searching. For instance, someone more visually-oriented would be interested in posing his victims like some sort of horrific and psychotic artwork, or taunting the police through letters. Somebody more auditory-oriented would like to hear his victims scream and beg, or he may call and taunt law enforcement. It turns out that most sexual serial killers are visual, with some, being sadists and having tendencies of wanting to see people suffer. They may also focus on a specific type of victim with certain physical features to satisfy a sexual fantasy in their mind. I have never found a serial killer to have a conscience or be empathetic. Instead, they tend to objectify their victims for their own extreme and distorted pleasure. Their focus is on immediate gratification, like a drug addict's, and what they can get out of torturing—sexually abusing and killing their victim of choice.

We learned that there are two types of serial killers. One type abuses substances, and the other is *clean*. This is interesting when it comes to what's known as the *cooling-off period* when a serial killer pauses or takes a break. What causes the cooling-off period? Why are there some serial killers who cannot stop? Nine times out of ten, the serial killers who can't stop are the ones abusing substances. When they ingest cocaine or alcohol, they become uninhibited. They can't control their urges nor do they want to, so they keep killing. And eventually, they get sloppy and get caught. Interestingly, I have never found serial killers who are sexual predators to be heroin addicts. If they were abusing heroin, their whole central nervous system would be completely depressed and in a stupor. They wouldn't have the angst. They would not have the mobility or the energy to be out hunting and killing.

We also determined there is a strong link to fetish addiction with serial killers. Many practice fetishes as part of their ritual—bondage, panty, foot, necrophilia, and on. There is an unbelievable emotional urge to act out this sexual fantasy with a body part or some physical object that is connected to sex. Often, the fetish is connected to having complete power and control over another human being. When it comes to necrophilia, there is obviously total control.

The vast majority of serial killers are not brain scientists. They're just guys who get away with murder in part because they're transient. Their whole murder ritual, from identifying and looking for a victim, to stalking that victim, to kidnapping that victim, to whatever their fetish is, and then killing that victim. This is their high: part of their addiction and part of their feel-good experience.

The bottom line is, the serial killer is out killing to feel good, but eventually, he's going to pay the price. Keeping that addiction going is a life of paranoia and horror because they're all afraid of getting caught. They need to live under the radar, work menial positions that never really amount to much, and attempt to keep their murderous thoughts at bay to remain in a neutral state of only fantasizing about their next victim.

At STALK, we endured a lot of rough years with no money, but we kept going on faith, care, and concern and the belief that we were helping people by saving a lot of lives. I really believe we did this simply by being out there publicly with our profiles—unlike the FBI who really won't put much out there for fear of being wrong.

STALK believed it was better for us to take our shot, and if we were wrong, then we were wrong. To be honest, I would rather have taken the chance on being wrong than miss an opportunity of being right and saving a life. That's the difference between STALK and a lot of other law enforcement organizations. We aren't concerned with public opinion. Because of my spiritual rebirth, I have to go to bed at night knowing I did the right thing and gave it my best shot, and I'm sure the rest of the team feels the same way.

Whenever we published a profile, the vast majority of the killing stopped. Some of STALK's profiles will be included in upcoming chapters. We understood we weren't putting the cuffs on anybody, but if we could flush the guy out and have him scared and on the run, then that was something. Serial killers don't feel empathy, sympathy, or compassion; but they do feel fear—big-time. They fear being apprehended and caged because they are all about power and control, and once they are caged, that's all out the window. There's no doubt we have saved lives, flushed these killers out, and neutralized them. Maybe they've moved on and killed somewhere else, or maybe they stayed frozen in fear. Serial killers are paranoid, and they are so narcissistic that they believe they are invincible and can evade being captured by law enforcement. They tend to constantly follow the news for all the information they can gather to see how close the cops are to apprehending them. STALK publicly puts the fear into these killers.

I was blessed by God in being surrounded by the talented people on the STALK team, trying to apprehend these killers and give those who were murdered a voice—as well as seeking some kind of justice for their families. The commitment, care, and concern are inspiring. You often hear the word *closure*. Let's try and get the guy and bring the family closure. There is no such thing. I've counseled a number of mothers and fathers who've lost kids over the years to violence or drugs, and they are left with a permanent hole in their hearts. You can help bring them some justice, which helps them cope with losing a loved one, but it never heals. The hole in their heart never heals.

CHAPTER 4

Interviews with Henry Lee Lucas and John Wayne Gacy

Henry Lee Lucas has been dead since 2001. Unfortunately, his name will not soon be forgotten. On January 11, 1995, I traveled to Huntsville Prison in Texas to meet with this twisted serial killer. My interview took place on death row, a bleak universe surrounded by concertina wire and prison guards in towers armed with rifles.

At the time of my visit, Lucas was on appeal for the murder of Orange Socks, an unidentified woman found in Texas on Halloween of 1979. When a criminal files an appeal, 99.9 percent of the time, he's not too willing to talk. So I was surprised that soon after reaching out to Lucas, I received his eager response.

Texas State Prison, Huntsville, TX

Dec, 22, 1994

Dear Mr. Kelly,

    I just received your letter telling me about your visit being approved.

    I'll be happy to see you. and I hope that you want be disapointed in our talk. I see that they set it on meda day, so it will be behind glass and screen and if you want to record our conversation bring a good tape recorder, it's hard to pick up one's voice through the screen. ok. I was looking for you in 93. I'm glad you could findly make the trip.

    Will that about all the time I have right now. I will be looking for you then.

    I wish you a very merry Christmas and the new year brings you happyness.

Sincerly,
Henry Lee Lucas

P.S. This Letter will give my permission To let you visit when ever you can come it hast to be on a Wensday from 9-11 AM so if something comes up you cant come on the 11 you can still come.

signed by
Henry Lee Lucas

Lucas was the first serial killer I had ever met with in person, and I had an immediate sense that he was somehow alien, that something vital was missing. Intellectually, I realized there was a man sitting before me, but my intuition told me this guy was not human. He had no heart, no soul, and no compassion. His glass eye reflected the flash from my camera, merely adding to his robotic presence.

Lucas was dying to talk, and he spewed out his unbroken thoughts for two hours. I had done my homework long and hard before ever even deciding to make this surreal visit. I had memorized the twisted events of this serial killer's life in an attempt to find some insight into the horrifying addiction of alcohol and killing innocent women.

Lucas was born in 1936, and over time had boasted of having killed upward of six hundred men and women, which prompted the formation of the Lucas Task Force in 1983; he was questioned regarding three thousand murders in over forty states. His fanciful confessions turned out to be an effective tool that allowed him to get out of prison on pleasurable road trips that included his favorite greasy fast foods, and he was able to do one of the things he loved best—talk ad nauseam about himself. His false confessions were also a devious way to mess with law enforcement. In the end, he was convicted of eleven homicides. Unfortunately, as is often the case, some law officials were all too relieved to close their unsolved murders. Lucas gave them the ability to clear the paperwork from their desks and feel a sense of closure and success.

When I first planned this trip to Huntsville Prison, I invited Marilyn to come along. However, she wanted nothing to do with visiting a serial killer, and who could blame her? So in her place, I invited a fourth-year Rutger's psychology student, Betsy, who had been working with me to accompany me and help with the interview, operate the tape recorder, and dress up a little to see firsthand how Lucas reacted live to an attractive woman. This was not the typical occasion a woman envisions wearing her little black dress, but it's also not every day a psychology student has the opportunity to be face-to-face with a murderous psychopath and renowned serial killer.

We flew out of Newark to Dallas a couple of nights before the interview, and my thoughts spun wildly having no idea of what to expect. This was a man who had committed numerous burglaries for which he served time, who had killed his mother during a disagreement (a crime for which he only served fifteen years of his sentence due to prison overcrowding), who begged not to leave the prison because he knew he would kill again, who had attempted kidnapping three young school girls, and who had also confessed to murdering his girlfriend—teenager Becky Powell—as well as an elderly woman he was caring for, Kate Rich, and who, in the end, was found guilty of a small fraction of murders he had boasted having committed.

Once we had settled in with Lucas, Betsy pressed record, and the tape spun quietly as Lucas spoke about his childhood, his alcoholic and abusive father, his abusive and disturbed prostitute mother, and his disdain for women. At that point, he said to me, "Mr. Kelly, when you leave, I'll remember you, but I got to forget about her" (referring to Betsy). That was my opening!

I asked, "Why, Henry?" His overt objectification of the female gender was all too real. His thoughts were chilling, especially delivered in his soft-spoken and rural-sounding diction.

Lucas: She could be the most odious thing you ever saw in your life. Wouldn't mean one thing to ya. Nothing. Just another pain in the side. She had to be gotten rid of or hit or something to get her away from ya. That's the way I was. Wasn't a good life, but it's what I learned to live with.

John: Could we go over what it was like with a woman and the anger inside? You talked about a deadness…

Lucas: A deadness. You could be around a person, and it's like that person's not there, but you still see 'em. Ya know what I'm sayin'? You gotta get away from her, and the more you try to get away from her, the closer she wants to become to ya. I honestly can't go, can't get away from her. It keeps eatin' at ya, ya know? You'll swing at her. You'll hit her…you'll kick at her. Like I said, I've slapped the devil outta some girls. I didn't mean it, but I did it. Get away from me! You have no control over it. Control is completely gone. It's something that just eats at you like a disease like I say, like a disease, it eats at you.

I've been in some awful fixes myself, ya know? Mentally fixes. That's what I call it—a mental blockness or whatever you want to call it. You have no compassion for nobody. No feelings. No compassion. Hatred. Real hatred, and that hate builds up. It eats at ya just like a cancer would eat at ya until it explodes. It's there—there every day. It's not something I can get away from, and I like to control my feelings about women, ya know the past year, but as far as trusting myself with women, I don't trust myself because I don't know what to expect from them. When I was staying with Becky (Powell, Otis Toole's mentally impaired teenage niece), I had to be around somebody else, ya know? With her, I couldn't be by myself. It's a feeling that you get. It's not safe to be with me. So keep her at a distance.

John: Is it a feeling of fear that she may do something that may cause you to act out, or is it a fear or rage for her?

Lucas: It's a fear of her. It's a female fear. You know what I'm saying? You see it. You know what happens, and you say, "Well, that's going to happen again," and you've got to block it out, or you don't survive. That's what I do. I block it out.

Lucas told us he was confident he would win his appeal. After all, he had not killed Orange Socks—though he had confessed to this particular crime on four separate occasions. I pressed him why had he admitted to all of these murders if he had not committed them. He glibly replied that hundreds of false confessions had gotten him out of prison.

"'If this was 1983, I'd claim these murders too," he would later brag to the *Houston Chronicle* in 1999. "I made the police look stupid. I was out to wreck Texas law enforcement."

I had spent a year arranging this taped interview, and I could not press too hard, but I still inquired about Lucas's relationship with Otis Toole, a major person of interest in the murder of John Walsh's son Adam.

"Otis and I are different because he liked those little boys. I don't know what he was doing."

In the end, what Lucas wanted most from me was a promise I would help secure six packs of cigarettes a day for his fierce habit. Ironically, he claimed smoking kept him from going crazy and killing someone. I kept my word and called the warden, "I'm a drug counselor. Can you let him detox in a humane way?" I asked for a nicotine patch or gum, but he let me know that Lucas's nicotine detox would amount to the last cigarette he smoked.

George W. Bush, governor of Texas at the time, ended up taking Lucas off death row for the murder of Orange Socks just fifteen hours before his scheduled execution; he was sentenced to life in prison for eleven murders. Lucas had told me, "I don't feel any guilt or remorse. I don't want to be famous for what I've done, but I am. I've been written up in books, and they even made a movie about me."

On March 12, 2001, Lucas died from a heart attack. He was sixty-four years old. His remains are buried in an unmarked grave in Huntsville, Texas.

John Wayne Gacy was the next imprisoned serial killer I thought of interviewing in the spring of 1993. Gacy was infamous and known as the "Killer Clown" due to his fondness for performing at parades, fundraisers, and children's parties as Pogo the Clown—his own invention. He was fifty-one years old when I reached out to him. In a mere thirteen months, he would be executed by lethal injection at Stateville Correctional Center in Illinois after fourteen years on death row, having been convicted of thirty-three murders of teenage boys, twelve for which he had been sentenced.

Between 1972 and 1978, Gacy had forcefully or deceptively lured his victims to his ranch-style home before sexually assaulting and torturing them. Most of his victims were strangled and buried in a crawl space in his Chicago house.

My objectives with Gacy were the same as they had been with Lucas. As an addiction specialist, I was trying to fit together the pieces of the puzzle. If I could interview Gacy as I had Lucas, I would gain deeper insight in the addiction of serial killing. After I had written to him, I received a bio sheet that he requested I complete before he grant me an interview as well as some propaganda he desired I circulate, testifying to his innocence.

```
                              John J. Kelly
                              201 Route 34
                              Matawan, NJ 07747
                              April 9th, 1993
Greetings Mr. Kelly,
I received your letter and with regards to your request for interivew
I will have to deny it.  .
Hwoever if you want to submit some questions in writing then I would
be willing to answer them as long as they don't deal with my case.
In doing so whenever I talk with anyone I like to know who that is and
some common facts about them enclosed is a bio sheet which you can fill
out and return with a photo and then I will send the same bio in the way
I answered it and it will give you some background.
my policy is simple no photo, no answer with bio sheet in full.
Thanks for your time.
The correct way to address letters to me is on the envelope. You can drop
the Mr Gacy as I am John or J.W. I am nobody important, just a man caught
up in the justice system.
                    take care for now,

                              Regards

                                       John
```

DISCOVERING LAZARUS

Bio Review

Full Name:_____ Date of Birth:_____

Age, HT., Wt.: _____ Home: _____

Maritial Status: _____ Family:_____

Wheels: _____ Brothers: _____ Sisters:_____

Most Treasured Honor:

Perfect woman or man:

Childhood Hero: Current Hero:

Favoirte TV shows:

Favorite movies:

Favorite song:

Favorite singers:

Favorite Musicians:

Hobbies:

Favorite Meals:

Why you wrote JW Gacy:

Recommended Reading:

Last Book read:

Ideal Evening:

Every Jan1st I resolve:

Nobody Knows I'm:

My Biggest regret:

It I were President I'd:

My advice to children:

What I don't like about People:

My Biggest Fear:

Pet Peeves:

Superstitions:

Friends like me because:

page two

Behind my back they say:

People in History I'd like to have met:

If I were an animal I'd be:

Personal goals in Life:

Personal interests:

Favorite color:_____   Favorite Number: _____

I view myself as:

What I think of this country:

Political views:

Thoughts on Crime:

Thougts on Drugs:

Thoughts on Sex:

I consider myself: Conservative _____ Moderate:_____ Liberal: _____
What I expect from Friendships:

Religious thinking:

What your thinking now:

Your artistic interests:

They Called Him The Killer Clown: But Is JW Gacy a Mass Murderer or Another Victim?

Questionable Conviction

John Wayne Gacy, convicted in 1980 of killing 33 men and boys, raises a number of provocative questions regarding his alleged crimes. An extensive study of over 15,000 pages of official records and transcripts leads to the conclusion that if you could take all of the facts and transcripts and feed them into a computer along with all of the Illinois laws, his conviction would be reversed.

Improper Confessions

Police claimed to have five separate statements from Gacy confessing to crimes. Yet none of these so-called confessions are signed. Three of them were taken orally and written up days later from memory and without notes. All of these statements were written by police in a self-serving manner.

Manner of Killing

Police claimed Gacy strangled all victims with a rope. However, Dr. Robert Stein, Cook County Medical Examiner, testified at trial that six deaths were caused by ligature strangulation, 13 by suffocation, one by stabbing, one by manual strangulation, and 10 undetermined.

River Victims

The cause of death of the two victims recovered from the river were listed on death certificates as unnatural drownings. The state claimed these were strangulations. However the Forensic Pathologist stated that for both victims, the neck area and the entire body were *atraumatic*, showing no evidence of injury that may have caused death.

Time Period

Gacy owned the house in Des Plaines for seven years. The state claims that the victims were killed and buried under the house over a six-year period, with most during the last four

FBI Criticizes Investigation

Special Agent Robert Ressler of the FBI's National Center for the Analysis of Violent Crime stated that Des Plaines police "did a sloppy job" of their investigation into Gacy's 33 alleged murders.

After focusing their investigation on Gacy, police failed to fully examine three other suspects. Nor did they correlate the disappearance of victims with Gacy's presence in Des Plaines.

years. Yet an expert from the Cook County Sheriff's office testified that the bodies could have been there anywhere from six months to ten years or longer. Anthropologists were never used to scientifically determine the actual length of time the bodies were buried.

employee who was believed to be involved disappeared and has never been found.

Records Destroyed

Gacy's work as a building contractor took him to 14 states, and in at least 16 cases, he was out of Cook County when the victims disappeared. This infor-

Only six were positively identified; identification of the rest was only tentative. Nine are buried in common graves with no identification at all. None of the families of identified victims received the entire bodies. The heads and hands were cut off and saved by the medical examiner's office.

> ## The question is, if Gacy was out of town when those murders were committed, then who did commit the murders?

Victim Connection

During nearly six weeks of trial, not one witness placed Gacy with any of the victims before, during or after the crime. The fact that Gacy owned or rented out the property does not necessarily mean he was the person who committed the crime or put the victims at that house.

Access to House

The house rented to PDM Contractors had 12 keys, many of which were held by employees with access to the property at all times. Keys to all vehicles and other business properties were similarly available to PDM employees. Two employees who had keys were given lie detector tests and failed them. Another

mation was suppressed at trial, and Gacy's business records documenting his absence from Chicago were destroyed by Cook County Sheriffs and the State's Attorney.

Drugs and Liquor

The State claimed that no drugs were found in Gacy's home. However, large quantities of Valium, Placidyl, Preludin and other drugs were removed from the house without being inventoried on the search warrants. The same is true with over 200 bottles of liquor and over 25 cases of beer.

Victim Identity

Nineteen of the victims were known to be male prostitutes.

Improper Procedures

On December 13, 1978, Gacy was illegally detained and abused by police for nine hours, and denied an attorney. On December 22, he was illegally arrested on a drug charge, kidnapped and brought to the police station. In June of 1979, Gacy was questioned for over three hours under the influence of truth serum. The results showed that he didn't know any more about the crimes than he had already mentioned. In August of 1979, defense investigators who had turned up evidence pointing to the involvement of others were dismissed.

There was no doubt Gacy was attempting to manipulate me, which was never going to happen. He seriously proposed that he had been illegally detained, framed, and that bogus drug charges had been filed against him. In addition, he claimed that the police had used a truth serum to coerce him into confessing. There was a sad absurdity in his fallacies and a total lack of responsibility for his killing spree. In any case, from our preliminary correspondence, without my meeting with him in person, I got what I needed. It was all too clear: this was a person with no guilt, no remorse, and no compassion. Without feelings for anyone, all he truly cared about was his own gratification.

Lucas and Gacy had both endured abusive childhoods and were both alcoholics who lacked the unconditional love and support needed to become healthy adults. Lucas had lost his eye when his prostitute mother attacked him with a broom; she also dressed him as a girl until the age of eight as well as forcing him to observe as she slept with her johns.

Gacy too was an unpopular and sickly child who was beaten by his alcoholic father. Gacy married twice but all the while led a secret homosexual life, and after he molested the wrong teenage boy in 1967, he was diagnosed with antisocial personality disorder. It's essential to remember that when most serial killers become violent sexual abusers, they are usually fueled by rage from their abusive childhoods. My interest was not what Lucas and Gacy or other serial killers had done but how they had gotten there. I was trying to assess the roles that not only drugs but also physical and emotional abuse play in a serial killer's development. About 95 percent of serial killers, including Gacy and Lucas, were raised by parents who abused alcohol and other drugs; these parents then passed the abuse onto their children.

In the end, I hoped my research would unveil ways to identify kids at risk for becoming potential serial killers, and if attempts at prevention failed, at least increase the chance of apprehension and arrest. I was concerned that less money was being allocated toward substance abuse treatment and that deficit in turn would lead to more addicted abusive parents, which could foster more serial killers. My favorite saying is, "Not everyone who is abused in childhood will become a serial killer. However, it seems every serial killer was abused in childhood."

Cocaine and heroin abuse was skyrocketing in the 1990s, and insurance companies were cutting drug treatment benefits by a large percentage. Without a doubt, being entrenched in the mine field of addiction meant understanding with horrific clarity how our country's well-being hung in the balance.

TEEN KILLER

Teen killer what have you done
Taking away life and innocence
She's laying face down in the morning
  sun
The darkness last night shivered
Through her heart with fear
You always enjoy that dance of lust.

To be sexually violent is orgasmic to you
The streets are filled with the missing
And the candles have been snuffed out
Society has been denied—No new stars
  tonight
In the sky only young heavens.

Feel free to take her blood-stained dress
She won't be needing it today
There's no prom now
Mother and Father wearing sadness
Will find a place for her to rest.

Your hunger is endless
You hunt like a predator
From the whipping post and lack of a
  nurturer
Her friends are playing alone now
Lots of time on their hands
Not knowing the clocks are running out
You're draining the sand
Life's dark only red-running streams
No joy in the park—Only in the rough-
  est of dreams

The night is coming—Time to dine
Another feast you shall have

Game is plenty from earth's young
  harvest
Troll your paths of lust and rage
Hurry midnight is coming
Self destruction turn the page

Your fear is growing—they're close at
  hand
Make friends with loneliness and cold
The grave is deep but shallow
You understand
There's nothing for us but hatred for you
You took away from her—You took
  away from you
Emotional specimens discarded by life
Fall victim to society's dumpster

Try not to wake up early and face the
  morning sky
It's too late for you—Here send your
  resume to God
There's nowhere to hide
The time is real, justice is now
These sins aren't forgiven by God
On the planet this isn't allowed
The chair is harsh—soon it will be over
Candeled out of pain and misery

Reflect on hatred and what it
accomplished
Lust, Rage, Violence and all that
bloodshed

CHAPTER 5

Green River Killer

If you are fortunate to live enough years and gain enough experiences, you may emerge with insights and the ability to glance back and apply all you've come to know to life moving forward. Only then do you get a glimpse of what is larger than us. Whatever your perception may be of the universe or God, as human beings, we never truly comprehend the meaning of it all.

For me, glancing back, there is a moment in time in 1982 that is proof of something at work so much greater than myself. This was a turning point. I was actually detoxing, pretty much a mess, living with my aunt in New Jersey and struggling to get my life under control in every way. My focus was to simply try and emerge from my stupor, to get myself back on my feet, and become employable, so I could make a living and pay my bills. This sounds so very basic, but it's a monumental feat when you're stumbling out of years of addiction.

I remember so clearly in freeze frames, watching the television during these days of slow healing; and various news stories were airing on the Green River Killer, horrific reporting on all the bodies being found in Washington State. The body count just kept adding up. I had no idea as I sat before the television, myself coming back from near death, hearing these brutal details of young women who would never get the opportunity I now had to reclaim my life and having no idea I would ever be a profiler or one day be involved in this terrifying case on the other side of the country.

Addiction problems are incredibly varied, but they share one insidious thing: the firm foundation of low self-esteem. As described in my book *Warning Signs*, "No matter what form it takes, the addiction controls behavior and overrides normal social instincts. Addicts will cheat, lie, steal or manipulate others in any way necessary to feed their habit."

Addictions are, in essence, obsessive-compulsive disorders. And whether it's through alcohol, drugs, sex, gambling, or killing, the negative emotions of low self-esteem and depression become mitigated, allowing the addict to feel more alive. Addiction does not find us from a place of strong self-esteem. "No self-obsessed stalker, no gambling addict, and no child addicted to violence ever became dangerous because he thought well of himself."

Addiction often progresses from an experimental and recreational phase to an abuse and dependence phase before blossoming into a full-blown disease. Some wonder if this line of reasoning acts as a measure of excusing the harmful actions of a person gone horribly wrong. But coming to understand addiction, even when it relates to an action as heinous as killing, is an attempt to help correct a destructive behavior before it ends in tragedy.

For me, the Green River Killer was the pinnacle of all cases—the most significant case happening at the time as well as the most notorious case in the history of the United States. To be asked to travel out to Seattle and to be involved and to offer my two cents on who the Green River Killer might be, this was all quite an honor. If I had been tapped on my shoulder in 1982, sitting in my aunt's home detoxing and be told, "Hey, John, one day, you'll be traveling out to Seattle, King County, Washington, and you'll meet with Frank Adamson, the longest-running commander in chief of the Green River Task Force," my reaction would have been pure hysterical laughter.

This was a major, major deal. Law enforcement was looking at forty-nine murders that they knew of—and they believed there was more than likely an equal number unknown out there. Female victims were being found up and down the Green River and all around Seattle. It's frightening to imagine, but it took twenty years to catch Gary Ridgway, twenty years for DNA progress to get to a point where they could get a match. The murders began in 1982. Gary Ridgway had become a murder machine.

Frank Adamson is a no-nonsense, incredibly knowledgeable, structured person. He was written up in *Life* magazine and was known as a cop's cop throughout the country. In April of 1986, at Quantico, Virginia Adamson gave a presentation to a class of F.B.I. "fellows" (homicide detectives chosen from throughout the country to profile serial murders) detailing the Green River Investigation, its management, and associated difficulties. He spared nothing. The Green River Task Force collected copious items of evidence from the murder sites filling a wall with black binders detailing the findings. The data from the binders including additional binders on the investigation of each victim and missing persons was then imputed into the master computer. During this process, Adamson chose four persons of interest for review.

When I arrived in Seattle, Adamson spent two days with me, showing me crime scene photos I was definitely not used to viewing: photos of the first four girls found in the Green River. These were victims who had been taken down into the river and were submerged with rocks placed on their bodies and even inside their genitals as weights. The killer arranged these victims under the water in pornographic poses, probably standing up on the riverbank to gaze down upon them under the rushing water to admire his perverse art. The bodies being underneath crystal clear water and the reflection of the moonlit sky enhanced and magnified his private and horrific pornographic gallery. The cold water served to preserve the bodies. This way, the killer could return to his crime scene and sexually pleasure himself while viewing his own evil handiwork. This was the beginning for Gary Ridgway. For me, seeing the photos of the crime scenes, the eerie images of these dead women, was shocking to put it mildly. No matter the mean streets from where I'd come, I had not seen such close-up grave and stomach-turning photos in my life.

From what I observed and learned in Seattle and from everything my training and experience told me, it seemed the person responsible for these unimaginably brutal and macabre crimes would be involved day-to-day as working with his eyes and his hands—a contractor or a carpenter for example. Adamson presented four or five people for me to sort through, and within this group was Ridgway. I left Seattle for the east coast and began sorting through and psychoanalyzing the persons of interest to determine which one could be the killer.

In the beginning, the Green River Killer stayed close to the river, but as the authorities moved in and focused on that area, he began to move to other rural areas, outside of Seattle, depositing bodies in clusters in mountainous terrain. Some bodies were found near the Seattle Tacoma Airport. Four or five bodies would be discovered, and then he would begin a new cluster. Considering the photos I had poured over, it was surprisingly strange that he was known to be a *soft* killer due to the way he strangled his victims. In many of the victims, the hyoid bone, a horseshoe-shaped bone in the neck between the chin and the thyroid, was not broken. The authorities believed he was adept at perfecting a choke hold. Unfortunately, most of the bodies found were nothing but skeletons since the killer was extremely proficient at hiding their remains. This meant the killer knew the terrain well. Some of the victims had to be maneuvered over steep slopes, seemingly inconceivable for one person to be able to handle alone, so we could not eliminate that there could be two people involved.

A detective from Los Angeles who was brought into the case by Frank Adamson was a firm believer in two predators being involved. The focus shifted to the terrain. This was in the northwest where hills are considered mountains on the east coast. How could he carry the bodies up these steep hills and slopes? From one particular dumping ground, the killer could view the entire city. This killer was a necrophilia who returned to the murder scenes to relive his darkest fantasies, having sex with these dead and decomposing women, staying with them all night. He was a very sick individual.

I continued to pour over the details of the case and was able to eliminate three out of the five persons of interest for Frank Adamson. The two who remained were Gary Ridgway and a trapper. Between the two, it appeared to me that the trapper was the guy we were looking for; he had grown up in an extremely abusive family. He had major issues with his alcoholic mother who drank throughout her pregnancy, having been taken away from her when he was just a baby and was placed in child care. The trapper had a history of killing animals and breaking laws, and because of his profession, he knew the area like the back of his hand. He was notorious for being cruel to women, and as far as I was concerned, he had no regard for women at all, sharing them with other men. I truly believed this was the guy since he had all the classic-serial-killer-risk factors.

Then there was Gary Ridgway who had a criminal record of having had sex with a prostitute who claimed he had choked her. She managed to get away. This was many years before the Green River Killings had begun. Gary Ridgway's mother had bailed him out, and that meant to me that she had some care and concern for him, so I assumed he had a decent relationship with her, and it was clear the trapper's relationship with his mother was anything but good. It was obvious that the guy killing these women had serious female issues, and the mother figure would be the culprit or the reason for the anger and rage. For these reasons, I eliminated Gary Ridgway and focused on the trapper.

Frank Adamson liked the work I did so much so that when he retired, he decided to come on staff at STALK as vice president; he also became one of the consultants for *Dark Minds*, a TV show I cohosted for the Discovery Network that featured unsolved murders, and, of course, many other cases. Years later, it would come out that the killer was Gary Ridgway.

FBI Profiler, John Douglas, had focused in on the trapper as well, so I was in good company being wrong. Other positives came from being consulted on this high profile case. Teaming up with Frank Adamson was such an honor, and this exposure led to being consulted on other prominent cases.

What did we all come to learn years later? There have been movies and documentaries and books written about the Green

River Killer. We are drawn to trying to comprehend how such a monster evolves. In part, we want to believe that in understanding what creates a serial killer, we will ensure it won't happen again. We analyze and comb over every gruesome detail, hoping to glean some sort of answer.

Gary Ridgway was born February 18, 1949, in Salt Lake City, Utah. He was one of three boys to parents Mary Steinman and Thomas Ridgway. Ridgway's mother was domineering, and his relationship with her was troubled. His low IQ made childhood more trying, having to repeat a grade due to poor performance. One of his first disturbing signs of violence, the experimental phase, was at the age of sixteen when he stabbed a six-year-old child after bringing him into the woods. His prophetic words, "I always wondered what it would be like to kill someone." The child survived. The foundation of child abuse, low self-esteem, and internalized anger leading to addiction is evident in Ridgeway's early life.

Ridgway joined the Navy after marrying his high school girlfriend, serving in Vietnam. He turned to prostitutes during this period, and gonorrhea was the result of unprotected sex, but he continued along his unsafe sex path, nonetheless. His first marriage ended after only a year. His second marriage was slightly different. Ridgway found religion and demanded his wife be equally devout while also having sex in public places or, unbeknownst to her, on the burial grounds of his victims. His second wife spoke of Ridgway having used a chokehold on her. All three of Ridgway's ex-wives spoke of his extreme need for sex, especially in the woods or out in public places. There seemed to be a dichotomy between his religious nature and his sexual nature, in particular, his need to solicit prostitutes. He and his second wife had a son in 1975.

Most of Ridgway's victims were believed to be runaways or prostitutes. His method of killing was by strangulation during the 1980s and 1990s, often returning to have sex with the bodies in the woods where he had dumped them. When he was first arrested in November 2001, he was convicted of killing forty-eight women; an additional conviction was added, bringing the count to forty-nine although he later confessed to approximately twice that number. Those who knew him best said he was an amicable man who seemed a bit different.

Ridgway received a sentence of life in prison without parole instead of a death sentence by entering a plea bargain and providing the location of some of the missing victims. Eventually, Ridgway confessed to seventy-one murders, but authorities believe the number is closer to ninety-one, most killed between 1982 and 1984 and picked up along the Pacific Highway South. He claimed to have killed so many women that he lost count. For a man who couldn't manage to perform well in school, he did manage to elude being caught for two decades and was keen enough to pollute his killing sites with items that didn't belong to him—like cigarette butts, gum, or writings, as well as moving some of his victims into the state of Oregon. All of his efforts succeeded in throwing off investigators.

He was arrested in 1982 for the solicitation of a prostitute, passed a lie detector test in 1984, and in 1987, the police took DNA samples from him which in 2001 led to his finally being caught—arrested as he was leaving his workplace, the Kenworth Truck factory. At the time of his arrest, he had been married for the third time for thirteen years. His wife had no idea of Ridgway's secret pastime which he boasted had been his *career*. Ridgway confessed to more murders than any other serial killer in the country though his victims were blurred in a sociopathic haze, faces, names, and burial sites indistinct for the most part. His confessional tapes are an evil glimpse into the mind of a demented madman who worked a job, was a husband, father, and neighbor. And somehow his lunacy was not detected by those who knew him in passing or those who knew him best. Ridgway confessed to having sex with his victims after they were dead, and he confessed to burying his later victims to prevent his necrophilia longings.

Scan Ridgway's victims' names, take the time to recognize how very young they were, visit the memorial websites their families have established in their memories. Like Tracy Winston, 1963–1983, a formidable little athlete and a young woman just on the cusp of beginning her adult life. Her photo is all contagious smile and promises of a bright future. Or Angela Marie Girdner, sixteen years old, baby faced with innocent blue eyes whose parents reported her missing in 1983. Ridgway explained to the authorities his *kind* or *gentlemanly* methods after picking up his victims, easing their nerves with soothing words to make them feel as though he cared. Only he didn't. One of his near victims, Rebecca Garde, witnessed Ridgway's change in demeanor after he had offered her a ride from work on a rainy Seattle night. Garde was miraculously fortunate, finding the strength to fight her attacker off and running to a nearby mobile home for help. Her survival story provides that horrifying glimpse, a shred of insight into the depraved mind of a serial killer.

Ridgway is spending the rest of his life in Walla Walla, Washington State Prison. I feel congratulations need to go to the fine men and women, alive and dead, who represented the Green River Task Force over the twenty years it took to convict Gary Ridgeway. They were the true heroes. And wouldn't you know, the Green River Killer is a model prisoner.

The Green River, Kent County

King County
Department of Public Safety
David G. Reichert, *Sheriff-Director*
W 116 King County Courthouse
516 Third Avenue
Seattle, Washington 98104-2312

August 7, 1997

John Kelly
Extracare Health Services
 Counseling Center
201 Route 34
Matawan, NJ 07747

Dear John,

Thank you for the information you faxed to me on July 25, 1997. I found your report very insightful, and it has rekindled my resolve to solve this case. I value the perspective you brought to the Green River investigation as an expert in the field of drug abuse and addiction counseling.

Thank you also for the your July 23, 1997 letter accompanying the report. There is really no need to write a letter to my superior as your kind comments are sufficient and very much appreciated.

I certainly enjoyed meeting you and will be in touch. Please don't hesitate to contact me at anytime.

Sincerely,

DAVID E. REICHERT - SHERIFF-DIRECTOR

Frank H. Adamson

Frank H. Adamson, Chief
Criminal Investigation Division

FHA:pm

CHAPTER 6

13

New York Times
METRO NEW BRIEFS: NEW JERSEY:
Backyard Grave Brings Arrest on Murder Charge
August 24, 1998

SOMERVILLE—A North Plainfield man has been accused of killing a woman and burying her in his backyard, Somerset County officials said yesterday.

The suspect, John Korman, 48, was arrested and charged with murder on Saturday evening after the police, acting on a tip, searched the backyard of his Harmony Street home and found an unidentified body buried in a grave, Prosecutor Wayne Forrest of Somerset County said.

Mr. Forrest described the body as that of a white female, between 20 and 30 years old, with brown hair and brown eyes. An autopsy was being performed yesterday, but the authorities said they suspected that the woman died from a blow to the head.

Only by living through trying times and somehow having the resilience to emerge do we later come to understand how these trials and tribulations have come to serve not only ourselves but also, thankfully, others. I never could have known as I sat in church that day, praying for God's assistance, that eventually, I would be able to help others after the frightening task of facing my own demons was laid to rest. Little did I know that I would be coming face-to-face with demons far more terrifying than my own, along this unexpected journey.

One such demon arrived on my doorstep after STALK was well underway. We share the same first name, and our birthdays are only a month apart, but our similarities end there. My thought was to enlist the help of John Korman or 13, as he was known on the show, *Dark Minds*, to build criminal profiles. I believe he was truly invested and wanted to catch these guys. When we first met, Korman was serving two life sentences for the murder of two women who were prostitutes. For the purposes of *Dark Minds*, he offered his *expert* opinion about the possible motivations lurking behind various cold cases. Any theories supplied by 13 were fueled by his own personal experiences, and his identity remained cloaked—his voice distorted for anonymity. Although his commentary was often brief, his few choice words were nonetheless both chilling and enlightening.

"This guy has a boat. He invites a young lady out on his boat. Where I'm telling ya, nobody can hear her scream," 13 offered, regarding the Atlantic City murders of prostitutes. Knowing the details of Korman's life, knowing he himself was the owner of a boat who took women many miles out in the ocean off the Jersey shore, made this theory all the more sobering.

"Can you tell me why this guy in Atlantic City strangled them and he didn't stab them, shoot them, hit them over the head? Why strangle?" I asked him.

"Let me see…When you strangle somebody that's close and personal, you can feel the life just flow out of the body. Also, he could strangle them because he knows he has to move the bodies and he doesn't want any blood in his car. I think he wanted to see his victims suffer, and I think he did that very well. That's it."

During the *Dark Mind's* show on the Woodsmen killer, 13 proposed a new theory. "I think these girls are all surrogates for somebody he has a lot of anger against."

"Talk about that anger that he has in himself," I suggested to 13.

"There's this dominant woman in his life," he responded.

"And she hurt him in some way?" I asked.

"She hurts him, belittles him. He just resents that so much. Of course, you know he probably hates himself too for allowing this to happen."

"Would you call him a hunter or a fisherman?" I asked.

"Yes, definitely," 13 agreed.

"Okay, what kind of a job do you think this guy had?" I asked. "What would give somebody time off from work?"

"Well, if the guy was a roofer, a rainy day would. I don't think steel workers or masons work on rainy days. Dry wall guys can't work or electricians. You got a lot of guys sitting in a gin mill, you know, depressed," 13 said.

"And the booze would uninhibit him…right?"

"Oh, that would encourage. You know this is just what everybody would think is—just an everyday guy. Now only the people really, really close to him may know that he may have a dark side."

When I suggested the Woodsman kills outdoor, 13 said, "Outdoor crime scene. Definitely. They go off to a secluded location to do what they do. Motel screams can easily be heard not to mention all the fingerprints and DNA that can be left behind. I think the woodsman is smarter than that."

"Why drug-addicted prostitutes?" I asked.

"They're easy. You know, you throw a twenty dollar bill at her or a fifty, and they'll go anywhere with ya."

Korman was just like other serial killers; he killed to live, and he lived to kill. He loved and craved excitement along with crack and booze. Addiction is never pleasant, whether it's the inability to resist food, drugs, gambling, or sex. But when addiction revolves around killing, this is a whole other dark universe that affects not only the addict but the helpless victims unfortunate enough to be encountered along the way. All serial killers are addicts, and they won't stop killing until they're caught or they die-although some do have long cooling-off periods. I have learned different things about the psychopathic criminal mind that I could not have learned in any classroom or in any books, and this has given me a better understanding of the predator being hunted.

There are essential aspects of Korman I came to know. Korman was a decorated Marine and a Vietnam vet. He said he joined the Marines at eighteen years of age; he wanted to go to Vietnam and kill some people. He consistently talked about the Marines having made him a trained killer. However, I don't believe this theory. They may have helped him excel at his deadly craft, but he was a severely abused and enraged young man when he enlisted. He had rules. He had to keep his power and his control in place, and we had to play the game. It was imperative for me to maintain intellect over emotion. He was and still is very important to me, all the information he has, and I could not or cannot allow emotion to destroy this relationship. I believe he was a prolific hunter of women in New Jersey.

This incarcerated killer and I have been playing mind games well over a decade. He is well aware that he's not getting any younger, and he's even more aware that he's not getting out of prison. He is hardened. No one can crack this guy. The frustration lies in knowing how resistant he is to give it up. I try to convince Korman that his best bet is to make the most of a bad situation. If he would give me something, some sort of an admission, his sought-after confessions would go a long way. Even Korman himself acknowledges that if he would give them up, his confession would have a tremendous impact, but this is a criminal who has not the slightest concern for his own redemption.

What does concern him are the seemingly small things that make his day-to-day life in prison more palatable. He enjoys receiving birthday and Christmas cards, money for phone calls, and food boxes; he likes receiving reading material. All of these perks make his existence less dreary. He truly has no one else caring on the outside. His family visits no more than once every two years. That's a lot of lonely time to pass.

My relationship with this killer has been a big piece of my life. A diabolical monster who is serving two consecutive life terms. Many of the cold cases in New Jersey bear his signature. I know he's a person of interest in the murders of two young girls who lived near him, as well as countless prostitute murders. These cold cases are in counties that run north to south and east to west throughout New Jersey. To hear Korman confess would shed long-needed light where there has only been grief and darkness. I have tried my best, manipulating him, after he tried to manipulate me into solitary confinement. He was then moved to a far less comfortable place in prison, but Korman is hard and tough. He understands a confession will mean better living conditions. However, he's at war with society and humanity. No matter what I have offered, a money, counseling and education for his children, or relocation to a cushy federal prison in Pennsylvania—nothing has made a difference to him, and nothing has been enticing enough to get him to talk. I can only keep working on Korman and hope something will one day come from this unlikely relationship.

This man is isolated and doesn't have anyone on the outside to depend upon. Over the years, our correspondence has led to boxes and boxes of letters, artwork, even crocheting and knitting, hardly the past times you'd envision for a brutal and twisted killer. He likes to draw, and like other serial killers, he's good at it. He's over sixty years old. He suffers from a heart condition, an aneurysm. He has recently had a stroke, and this means that time is running out. Why this criminal has latched onto me is complicated. In a strange way, even though we are the same age, he seems to need a father figure, the emotional connection to someone he respects on the outside. But no matter our emotional connection, Korman cannot conceal his true nature from me. When you are in the presence of this man, there is no denying that beneath his skin lurks a monster, an admitted sadist. Much of my insights have come from our face-to-face visits, along with the written and phone conversations. During my first visit with him in prison, I felt that he was robotic—a true conglomeration of evil.

"You see that girl over there?" he asked during this visit. I glanced over at another table and found a sweet young girl sitting with her incarcerated father. Before I even had a chance to respond, Korman continued, "When I see her…I see a victim."

I will never forget this conversation; his matter-of-fact words were so scary, and he was dead serious. This was not a prostitute he was eying but a child. This means Korman could have targeted young girls before. And two of the girls murdered, ages fourteen and fifteen, were from the vicinity where he lived. We are attempting to reopen these cold cases with law enforcement. Somehow in the evidence room, there may be DNA that would prove his guilt. If he spills his guts, he would be moved. These types of crimes against children would put Korman at risk of violence from the other prisoners.

Working with Korman is a major cat-and-mouse mind game in progress. And for me, it's also a spiritual awakening in the process. This is the impetus behind my offering money to his family upon his death, to bury him where he wants in the hopes that he would place more value on helping his family financially than maintaining his stony silence. In my opinion, Korman is more than likely the most prolific sexual predator in the history of New Jersey. Every serial killer has a signature, and it's my opinion that Korman's shows he was incredibly active; I would guess, based on our mind games, with at least twenty-four bodies in New Jersey and the metro area.

Much of my insight has come from our in-depth correspondence, either by phone or mail. The excerpts that follow are pulled from Korman's letters and span many years and illustrate the depth of his mental illness. It's hard to imagine this man as an innocent little altar boy who may or may not have been sexually abused. Some of Korman's letters are less frightening than others, but the overall effect will leave you cold. For those who would rather not enter the mind of a depraved serial killer, you may want to forgo reading the following section. For the more hardy souls, you will gain a glimpse into a twisted mind that you may never have had the opportunity to experience.

I will be happy to help you out any way I can. When I read the pages you enclosed with your letter is was as if someone reached into my mind and stole my childhood. I was abused by both mother + father. My dad was an alcoholic. He worked 3rd shift at the Mack motors in Plainfield, NJ. He took

a three inch lether belt and with a razor blade cut it into a seven stran whip. He would whip us if we woke his sleep.

After the divorce Mom took over as the ridget disiplinarian. She would Beat me with a broomstick braking it most of the over my back. Mom Never drank.

To back-up a bit I was first introduced to alcobol as a baby. Mom or dad used whiskey on our gums to relieve teething pain. Later I learned he would put half a shot of whiskey in our Baby bottles to assure a good nights sleep.

In my early teens in JR. High school I can remember cutting school, going over to a friends house, whoses father had a bar ,and drink the day away. Alcohol has always been a part of my Life. It was Like a Love affair. As I grew so did my love for alcohol.

After being married for twenty-four years my wonderful wife could'nt take my drinking anymore. I think it was being away from her coaxing me that led me to drinking out-of-hand, prostitutes, and crime. After we split I started messing with fast woman, that only led me to drugs, I picked-up a crack cocaine habit fast. for the next 6 yrs, it was in and out of the V.A. hospitals drug + alcohol programs

I would not survive another bout with drugs.

So MR. John Kelly— this is a quick summery of my life. If you wish to visit or corrispond, Like I said earlier, I will help in every way.

I am, however, trying to get my plea back so I may have to limit my answers.

Hope to hear from you.

Sincerely yours,

John Korman

PS. Please call me John.

August 26, 2013

I still see *P* at veteran meetings. It's hard to pump him for information, but I'm working on it. I thought for sure he would speak easily about his crimes, but he's finding it hard. "There's some things better left unspoken," he would say, or "Some secrets should die with me."

The Fly on the Wall

Ever since I came to Trenton State Prison, I dove into studying law, trying to find the smallest loophole that would reduce my culpability for my two separate murders and perhaps, one day, walk the streets a free man. But sentenced to two thirty-to-life terms, my parole date is 2057, putting my age at 117 years old before making parole. I doubt very much if I'll ever be a free man again.

Was it my post-traumatic stress disorder talking to me? The fact that I had pounded into my head in boot camp over and over that a marine is a lean, mean, killing machine, and began to actually believe it, or was it my very own psych trying to keep me sane? Perhaps it's easier to believe I was a killing machine than accept the fact that I could kill so easily and break down crying at the atrocities of my actions. If you've ever been in a veteran's hospital and noticed the men walking around the halls in what seems like a daze, you'll understand how someone can disconnect with life itself.

When people ask, "Did you kill anyone in Nam?"

I would answer *yes*. That question, for some reason, was always followed by, "How did it feel to kill someone?"

Even today, right now, I don't know how to answer that question. In the past, I would boast of my kills and how exciting it was to get one of those gooks in my sights (which, by the way, were very elusive). To pull the trigger and see him fall, it had to be one of the most exciting things in my life.

Yeah! I would think to myself, *Got that bastard.* But today I don't brag. I think how insensitive I felt back then. These enemy I killed were someone's father, brother, or son. And that kind of eats me up inside. Again, today I keep asking myself why I survived and so many others, others better than me did not. Yet there is a part of me that still thinks it's cool as ever to kill. That sense of godliness you feel; just like being back in Nam. And still I search for the answer as to *why* I feel this way.

*****

At this point, it's important for you to understand how I met Korman. We, STALK Inc., were invited in to do a profile on the Tamara Tignor murder by the BridgeWater police. A drug-addicted prostitute from Newark, New Jersey was found murdered in a park in affluent Bridgewater, New Jersey. At that time, there was a major investigation going on in Newark for the murders of countless prostitutes over the years. It is also important for you to understand the trap I set for Korman. When I first went to see Korman in prison, I asked him how many total kills he had. His answer was fifty-four. Then I asked him, "How many people did you kill in the US, and how many did you kill in Vietnam?"

His answer to me was, "You're the profiler. You figure it out."

I waited a year. During that period, I gained better rapport with him over the phone on weekly calls. Then when I went to visit him. I asked him how many kills he had in Vietnam. I was hoping he forgot about our last conversation on the topic a year ago. I was right. He did forget.

He answered, "I had twenty-eight kills in Nam."

So I thought to myself, *Okay, John. That leaves twenty-six murders here.*

Finally I confronted him on his kills. This was his response:

October 15, 2014

About my fifty-four kills. Ever since I came back from Nam, I've had my death toll at several different numbers. Within a year or two, I settled on fifty-four. It seemed like a believable number. I guess I was correct. But the God's honest truth, I'm not sure what the real count is, probably closer to twelve or thirteen. So please, John, put your overactive mind to rest. There are no *others* to concern ourselves about. And you, John Kelly, after all these years, you still don't believe me. That feels like a knife in my back.

John, there's an old Marine Corps part of me that loves to brag about my many battle-field-confirmed kills. Even before I enlisted, I often wondered what it would be like to take a life. I'm sure every man on this planet thought it one time or another.

Then one night while with a hooker, a fear, like no other, comes over me. And the only thing I can connect that fear with is the fear of being in Nam, and that split second a bullet cracks over your head. (Oh, shit. An ambush!) And you know you're about to die. Then that *fight or flight* mechanism kicks in, and before I knew it, I was reaching for a gun; and oh no, there's a dead hooker lying there. Why did I do that? I still tell myself "I don't know."

Mix that old marine with several kills with all the shit he put up with as a kid, and you have a cocktail for a lethal man.

Sometimes, I wonder if all the miles of jogging in boot camp, singing to the drill instructors rhythm. Then for the next one fourth of a mile every time your left foot hit the ground, the DI would yell *kill*, and the next time your foot hits the ground, you holler *kill*.

Before you know it, you're yelling, "Kill, VC, kill, NVA, kill, kill, kill." Not that little boy in be that wonders what it would be like to take a life is transformed into someone that cannot wait to pull the trigger on some gook. Yeah! That little boy inside me is screaming out *killl!* Then that *kill-crazy* kid returns home.

So look, John, I wish I could bulls——t around and plead to the Tignor murder. Somewhere in that perverted little mind of mine, that would be one more notch in my M16. But the truth of the matter is even if I did cop out to it, I'm sure the prosecutor will ask me questions only the real killer can answer.

As for me, everything is okay. Now that I'm back in the South Compound, I have a window with a view to see the fireworks at midnight. So I'll try to call on Sunday night.

As always,

John

Hey, Big Daddy, What's Up?
October 18, 2010

It's very easy for law enforcement to try to pin other unsolved murders on a man that almost mirrors his crime. When I was arrested, there were eight or nine unsolved homicides in Newark, New Jersey, all prostitutes that the county detectives formed a task force and tried to pin 'em on me. Thank goodness that guy was caught.

But the big question is: Does this man have other crimes, and how can we get him to admit them? The police came to me and wanted me to get any other crimes I committed *off my chest* and to give closure to the families. Are you friggin' kidding me? I couldn't care less for the families. Shame on them for allowing their daughters to lead that kind of lifestyle and closure—all the cops wanted was to pin another crime on me.

This was not an accurate statement, John, made about one guy being responsible for all the murders in Newark, New Jersey. Some were solved. The vast majority were not, and there was a hell of a lot more than eight or nine women murdered.

*****

There is no surprise after reading Korman's letters and glimpsing his disdain for the female gender, his disregard for prostitutes and the families of prostitutes, and his unusual concern for his own family and not wanting to cause them any further shame or sorrow that he would be unwilling to offer any confession to those who lost a young daughter, a sister, a friend, or mother.

New York Times—
NJ LAW
NJ LAW; Series of Killings? Yes. One Serial Killer? No.
November 29, 1998
By Andrea Kannapell

In August, the police, acting on a tip, had unearthed the body of yet another woman, who had been bludgeoned. The body, buried in the backyard of a North Plainfield man, was identified as that of Nancy Nott, 21, of Plainfield, in Somerset County.

The police arrested the man, John Korman, 48, and later the authorities seized a fishing boat owned by Mr. Korman and his brother, James, looking for ties to a body found in Raritan Bay in 1995. The Somerset task force is looking into that case, according to a statement by the Somerset Prosecutor, Wayne J. Forrest, because "recent developments have indicated that the victim may have been in the Somerset County area at or about the time of her death."

Star Ledger
September 3, 2008

A Superior Court judge today refused to grant another trail to a North Plainfield man who admitted murdering two women, but claimed his lawyer failed to properly defend him.

Judge Edward Coleman sent John Korman Jr., 58, back to state prison to continue serving his sentence for the deaths of Plainfield residents Paula Strazdas, 34, and Nancy Nott, 21. He pleaded guilty to murder in 1999.

Korman said his former lawyer, Michael Rogers, coerced him into pleading guilty, failed to pursue a diminished capacity defense based on his post-traumatic stress disorder and refused to provide him with all of the evidence from his case.

Coleman said Rogers was more credible than Korman when they testified last month. During an Aug. 18 hearing, Rogers told the judge he took Korman's post-traumatic stress disorder into account, but did not believe it would have been enough to prove a diminished capacity claim.

In his ruling, Coleman said, "this is the type of advice an attorney is expected to give clients." He added, the "defendant appears to have mistaken honest opinion for ineffective assistance of counsel."

The judge also agreed with Rogers' decision not to provide Korman with copies of some evidence, and called it a sound, tactical decision. Other inmates were trying to gain access to Korman's information—statements, photos and police reports—and were volunteering to testify at Korman's trial.

Coleman said that there is no evidence indicating Rogers pushed Korman into pleading guilty. When Rogers told Korman he would face the death penalty if he proceeded to trial, that wasn't a treat, it was an evaluation, Coleman said. "The defendant was facing death."

Korman admitted shooting Strazdas twice in the head in 1995 and previously told the judge he struck Nott with a baseball bat in 1998. He previously tried to withdraw that plea, but the judge refused, calling it a late change of mind. He sentenced Korman in May 2000 to more than 93 years in prison, under a plea deal that spared him the death penalty.

Korman's attorney, Michael D'Anton, said his client plans to appeal this morning's decision.

One neuropsychologist, Ferguson, has written a book on the sociopathic gene. If you have this gene and you're raised in a rotten family like Korman was, you become engulfed with internalize rage that you long to take out on others. I mean, at eighteen years old, Korman couldn't wait to join the marines and kill somebody. He told me, "I had to get off on somebody. That's why I wanted to go to Viet Nam."

He described how he shot families walking down the street for no reason at all. Is this true or not? I have no reason not to believe him because he is so matter-of-fact. Korman has nothing to lose. He knows he's going to die in prison for what he's done. He knows I'll make sure he's cremated and his ashes are tossed in the ocean—even though he's not been honest about all the murders he's committed. You know, people have come up to me and said, "How can you go into the mind of a serial killer?"

My usual answer is, "As long as I don't let the serial killer go into my mind, I'll be okay."

I was talking to Korman one night not so long, and I said to him, "John, were you ever shamed as a child, young adult, did you ever feel you were being made fun of, humiliated, or ashamed?"

There was quiet over the phone, and then he answered, "Yeah, when I beat Nancy Knott to death with the baseball bat. I couldn't get an erection and felt like she was making fun of me. And she said she had to go. And I didn't want her to go until I got an erection. I was feeling humiliated, so I beat her to death with the baseball bat." This was the first murder for which he was caught.

Later on in another conversation, I asked him about remorse. I said, "People like you supposedly don't have the ability to feel remorse."

Korman responded, "Yeah, John, I really don't feel remorse." He really doesn't. He doesn't have a conscience. And if you don't have a conscience, how do you have a soul?

I asked, "Did you ever feel bad about anything?"

He thought for a moment and then said, "The only thing I ever really felt bad about is getting caught for what I did."

I asked Korman, "Why not come forth and collect the fame for being the most prolific killer in New Jersey history?"

And he replied, "In order to become famous I would have to admit to murders, and I won't do that."

Korman remains in prison, holding on to the one thing he has control of that others so desperately want—his confessions. We continue to play our mind games for opposite reasons, but both of us are equally vested, and sadly time is running out.

JOHN KELLY

Judge grants North Plainfield man new hearing in 1999 murders

Posted by kheyboer May 28, 2008 14:48PM

Patti Sapone/The Star-LedgerJohn Korman Jr. prepares to leave the courtroom in Somerville today at the end of his session.

A North Plainfield man who is seeking a new trial in the deaths of two Plainfield women will get a hearing on some of the issues surrounding how previous attorneys handled his defense.

Superior Court Judge Edward Coleman this morning agreed to grant John Korman Jr., 58, a hearing to determine whether his lawyer coerced him into pleading guilty in 1999 to the murders of Paula Strazdas, 34, and Nancy Nott, 21.

The judge also will hear evidence on whether Korman received access to all the discovery in his case and the discussions behind the attorneys' decision not to mount a defense based on his post traumatic stress disorder.

Paula Strazdas and Nancy Nott

Korman appeared in Somerville alongside his current defense attorney, Michael D'Anton, who said his client always wanted to go to trial and still does, knowing the state will not offer him another deal. The one Korman received in 1999 spared him the death penalty.

Somerset County Assistant Prosecutor James McConnell noted that Coleman was the judge who took Korman's original guilty pleas and twice determined that the defendant entered those pleas "truthfully and voluntarily." He also questioned Korman's motives for raising the issue now that the death penalty is "out the window." The state Legislature abolished capital punishment in December.

Star-Ledger photo of John Korman leaving
Somerville, NJ courtroom in 2008

CHAPTER 7

Ghosts of Mississippi

C olumbus, Mississippi, is a city just above the Tombigbee River. Some locals still consider Possum Town to be its name, dating back to the Native Americans pre-1821. This sleepy southern community is steeped in history; the origins of Memorial Day were believed to have taken root here, and during the Civil War, thousands of casualties were transported and buried in Friendship Cemetery.

A group of women decorated both the Union and Confederate graves with flowers, their gesture immortalized in a poem by Francis Miles Finch, "The Blue and the Grey." Columbus was spared from being burned to ash, unlike many of its neighboring southern cities during the Civil War. Historically, Columbus has distinguished roots. But in more recent times between late 1997 and 1999, the community found its way into the news due to the tragic murders of five elderly people. This eighteen-month period scarred the town and cast a pall in the southern air.

In 1999 when I heard of the five elderly murders in this small college town, I truly hoped and believed STALK could help, and this prompted me to phone Detective Gary Moore to see if they wanted us to work on a profile. It seemed Detective Moore was overwhelmed; the police department recently increased the reward for the killer, and they were receiving hundreds of leads.

I was eager for STALK's involvement with this high-profile case, just as I had been eager to help out in Seattle with the Green River Case. I learned all I could about the five victims: Mack Fowler, seventy-eight years old, a retired farmer, stabbed and strangled on July 8, 1996; George Wilbanks, seventy years old, an interior decorator, stabbed and strangled on November 2, 1997; Robert Hannah, sixty-one years old, a retired cafeteria worker, gagged, strangled, and his house set on fire on October 13, 1998; Louise Randall, eighty years old, a retired grocery store owner, bound, gagged and strangled on October 20, 1998, and Betty Everett, sixty-seven years old, a beautician, bound, gagged, and strangled on November 17, 1998.

Detective Moore spoke to his chief, and they invited me to fly out to Columbus. I took a jet to Atlanta then a puddle jumper to Columbus. When I arrived, the town was getting really kind of crazy—people buying guns, arming themselves in this very intimate town in Mississippi of about thirty thousand.

There was good reason for the escalating fear. Police Chief Donald Freshour said himself, "Once you get a dog started killing, eaten chickens...you don't stop." Hearing words like these spoken by local law enforcement had an obvious effect.

The people of Columbus not only took up shooting, but they were told, "Don't shoot at the legs...shoot to kill." No surprise, they also began locking their doors. The community understood all too well that the killer was staying one step ahead of law enforcement.

No one likes to imagine innocent folks being killed in their hometown, but when those folks are the elderly, when someone invades their homes with no forced entry, and all the victims live within a few miles of each other, something inconceivable and unsettling registers in the collective mind-set. Four of the five victims were strangled. All were elderly, cruelly murdered where they should have known no fear and no harm. Robbery seemed to be the apparent motive, but I had to make sure. These poor seniors were the victims of diabolical evil.

Detective Gary Moore—a big, tall, southern man, cowboy boots, and all—met me at the airport. Moore was the detective who introduced me to this case. He seemed extremely professional and passionate about solving it. I could tell he was a good and determined man. He drove me to my hotel, discussing the horrific details along the way. I struggled, trying to get a good night's rest. And the next day, he brought me to the crime scenes.

Columbus struck me as a sweet town with friendly people and attractive mansions on Main Street—its quaintness only made it all the more inconceivable to imagine these crimes.

We began with the houses of the two elderly women, Louise Randall and Betty Everett. Both were found tied with similar knots and strangled. The gas was turned on in each of their homes. After they were tied up and gagged, they were more than likely approached with a gun or a knife and told they needed to reveal where their money and valuables were hidden. Betty Everett complied as her money and jewelry were taken. Her house was meticulously combed through, not ransacked.

Louise Randall was a tough woman and never gave up the whereabouts of her money. Her son, Grady, was questioned regarding her murder. In time, however, Grady Randall cooperated with the authorities and passed a lie detector test. Grady Randall thought his mother's house had been staged; he claimed a stranger's keys were found at the crime scene.

These murders were not sexual. They were clearly about money. More than likely, we were searching for a *comfort* killer—one who kills for money or valuables that he can use to take care of his creature comforts—like a drug addict who kills for money or for drugs. From my personal experience with drugs, from my educational and professional years spent focusing on addiction, I had clear insight into what this meant. The addict will take dangerous risks to support his or her habit. These risks can take many insidious forms—lying, cheating, stealing, and most tragically, killing. All these risks are taken to acquire money to feed the addiction. We felt these were the motives that inspired the killer, so this became our focus. I knew that the residents in Columbus were frightened, and they believed the killer was a local, someone who lived among them. There's nothing worse than living in fear and to be constantly glancing over your shoulder.

A panel was put together to focus and brainstorm to see if we could figure out who this person might be. The brainstorming panel was comprised of about eight to ten people who met in the courthouse the day before I was to leave Columbus. What struck me as strange, I was surrounded by local detectives, and state police detectives but no FBI. This was something that bothered me right from the beginning. Why were the FBI profilers not called in, and, more importantly, why was STALK involved instead? Being asked to participate in such a high-profile case was, of course, exactly what we hoped for, and we were honored. But STALK was an unknown organization from New Jersey. There was no way I could proceed blindly and not question why we were asked to come down to Mississippi to do a profile on this case when all the chief of police had to do was pick up the phone and call the FBI for assistance.

I sat with this round table panel and tried to put the pieces together, knowing all too well that a lot of municipalities care an awful lot about their turf—territorial is the operative word. The reality is, the chief of police, Donald Freshour, was the one who would make the call about which law enforcement were let in and which were not. My experience out in Seattle had been entirely different. My partner Frank Adamson had invited whomever he could for fresh eyes on the Green River case in the hopes of finding a solution. But as I was sitting around this panel, listening to the talking going on back and forth, it was painfully obvious this case was not being run in the same manner. There were no FBI agents present.

At a certain point, the press was asked to leave the room, including *48 Hours.* Harold Dow, an award-winning journalist and a real nice guy and gentleman, was there as well as the producer, the sound man, and camera man. Really all nice professional people. This was my introduction into the world of news and show business. We had some surreal conversations when we were talking about the murders of the elderly and how could we catch this killer. They were good people. Unfortunately, the whole *48 Hours* team, as well as a couple of other reporters, were escorted out the door. The panel insisted on privacy. That meant no media.

The whole scene felt a bit crazy. Why was the media not notified sooner? There was this young woman from a local Mississippi newspaper who claimed she had the constitutional right to remain. And of course, they ordered her to leave, which led to an argument between this young reporter and the powers that be. She was informed that she would be arrested and brought down into a jail cell in the bowels of the old courthouse, but this didn't faze her. She continued protesting, and then she was taken away crying. Little did I suspect that things were going to get even more insane.

The next day, I said goodbye to Detective Moore and the district attorney before boarding a plane and flying home with the producer from *48 Hours.* In the days that followed, my team at STALK and I put our heads together and compiled all our evidence. And after a lot of work, we had our profile complete. The killer more than likely was part of the Columbus community. Since there had been no forced entries, the victims more than likely let him in on their own accord. The fact that this person was methodical (his knot-tying reflected this) and organized were also clear. He was shrewd at leaving not a trace.

We sent the profile out to Columbus, and then some months passed. All of a sudden, we heard the chief of police ended up getting arrested, and it came to be known that he was being investigated by the FBI. Now it all made sense why there was no FBI involvement. While the investigation of the elderly murders was going on, the FBI was doing their own undercover investigation of the police chief due to suspicion of his taking taxpayer money that had been earmarked for helping to solve other crimes, like the murders. He was giving his girlfriend a good deal of money from this government subsidized fund— crime-stopper tip money—most definitely not an upright thing to do. No surprise that he ended up being charged, convicted, and sent off to prison.

Incredibly, the chaos did not end there. When the chief of police was arrested, as crazy as it seems, some of the detectives who were working the case and detectives I had been working with were put on the street and turned into regular-uniformed police and traffic cops. They then took some of the police officers and traffic cops working the streets and turned them into detectives. Well, at this point in time and as far as I was concerned, the whole case fell apart. Now you had inexperienced cops working as detectives and trying to catch a serial killer, and all the seasoned detectives who were working with the chief were handing out tickets and working the streets. One thing is certain: someone had informed on the chief for taking all of the tip money.

When the chief talked on the news about the killings before we got there, the very next day, another victim, Betty Everett, was found as if Freshour was being publically taunted.

After the chief was charged and convicted of pillaging the money and giving it to his girlfriend, on June 26, 2000, *The Ghosts of the Mississippi*, an investigative report aired, delving into the five murders of senior citizens between late 1997 and early 1999. This was the first *48 Hours* on which I appeared, and by the time the show aired, the police chief was out of prison after serving eight months and was putting his life back together.

"I'm still human, and I screwed up," he explained to the less-than-pleased community. Freshour turned to construction work and left the police force. The whole experience was just out of control. This whole case blew up and went cold. All those murders went cold for all those years, from 1996 until 2012, when two arrests were finally made.

While working on *Dark Minds* with the Investigation Discovery Network in 2011, I spoke to 13 about the Columbus, Mississippi, murders to see if he had any insight to offer. Our objective was to update our profile of the suspected killer in the hopes that the public would be able to help with the identification. Oh what the hell. If your after a diabolical killer, you might as well consult a diabolical killer to see who he thinks killed these people. I asked 13 why someone would be interested in killing the elderly.

He answered, "Money. These people were tied up and gagged. Okay, he probably did that to search the house for money. Or something he could sell. I wouldn't be a bit surprised if these people were murdered shortly after the beginning of the month when they got their welfare checks. In the group that I hung out with, the ladies called that their Mother's Day gift. You know, the girls on welfare. They get their Mother's Day present on the first of the month."

"Tell me what kind of guy murders these elderly people," I asked 13.

"Somebody who works in an old folk's home maybe or delivers food to these elderly."

"Do you think he was a drug addict?"

"Good possibility. I've seen good people that turn to drugs, and their entire attitude changed. You know…they would do things that they never thought they would do."

"There was no sign of any break in, so what does that tell you?" I asked 13.

"That she knew her killer."

"Was this guy getting a sexual high by tying them up?"

"No, that's just a to-keep-her-there while he's searching for the money," 13 responded.

"Do you think he may have tied them up and kind of tried to scare them into telling him where they may have had a good bundle of their money hidden?"

"Oh yeah," 13 agreed.

"I don't think this guy was a thrill killer or a rage killer," I determined.

While the crew was in Columbus shooting *Dark Minds*, one of the original law enforcement officers who worked on the murders back in the 1990s gave us some further insight.

"When it began, it was just another murder. We go out, we process the crime scene, we do investigative leads, and then another murder occurred before we could solve the first murder. And then another murder occurred…the town was literally turned upside down."

It's hard for me to believe that somebody would stage a murder and make it look like a robbery to spend all that time, risking being caught not knowing if someone's going to come in and check up on these elderly people. I believe the motive was the same at least for both of the elderly women victims— money. Whoever killed these women, I truly believe it was about the cash.

The crime lab in Mississippi offered further insight. It was indicated how state-of-the-art technology was being utilized.

Their forensics confirmed that the first two murders were not connected to the other three. It was inferred that at least one in the remaining three cases may not be connected either.

"From analyzing the crime scenes...you're able to see some glaring dissimilarities between these two cases. In some cases, the offender may have been a little more organized whereas other crime scenes present more of a disorganized feel—which is one of the things that leads us to believe that these cases are not as connected as some people think."

The crime lab believed some of the crime scenes may have been staged while others seemed more opportunistic in nature. Forensics certainly helped move the investigation forward. It's easy to look back and find all the glaring mistakes that were made. The Columbus Law Enforcement later admitted their mistakes that the crime scenes were "tainted and trampled" and that more care should have been used. No matter what and no matter the time that elapses, the evidence that is lost and the possible witnesses who have moved or passed away, murder cases are never closed.

More than a decade after the first elderly murder, an arrest was made in February of 2012. Columbus Police Chief Selvain McQueen, whom I remembered as a real dedicated detective years before when I was down there, arrested Earnest Terell Talley, forty-four years old, for the murder of George Wilbanks in 1997.

Chief McQueen had been on the Columbus Police Force all those years ago when Wilbanks and the other four seniors had been killed, chasing leads that never amounted to anything. In 2012, Talley had been in the Lowndes County Adult Detention Center for a month on a burglary charge. Talley and

Wilbanks had shared mutual friends back in the late 1990s. At the time of Talley's arrest, authorities would not disclose his motive but told the media, "It has to do with money, but as far as details, we'd rather not say anything."

Police Chief McQueen gave credit to investigator Cockrell as well as two retired officers, Williams and Bowen, for coming out of retirement to work on the cold case. McQueen never believed the elderly murders were committed by a serial killer. As reported by Carmen K. Sisson of *The Dispatch* in February of 2012, McQueen stated, "It feels good bringing closure for the family of the victim." He pledged "without a shadow of a doubt," there would be additional arrests for the other tragic murders.

Five months later, in July 2012, Curtis Hinton turned himself in and was charged with capital murder for the death of George Wilbanks. Investigators believed Hinton and Talley committed the murder together. At the time of Hinton's arrest, his wife, Laura Hinton, claimed Hinton was innocent and had an alibi. She was shocked that her husband was arrested despite his past criminal history, fully believing he had *cleaned his life up*.

According to Laura Hinton, her husband and George Wilbanks were friends, and Hinton working as his gardener before they ventured into interior design work with one another. Wilbanks even attended Hinton's previous wedding. Apparently when her husband was struggling with drug addiction, he and Talley did crack together on occasion. She doubted

Talley's honesty and felt the police in Columbus were simply wanting to wrap up a cold case. "They're trying to convict an innocent man," she claimed.

Ernest Talley ended up being sentenced to ten years in prison for burglary charges; he had been arrested thirty-one times since 1997 back when the elderly in Mississippi were being killed. In August of 2012, the grand jury refused to indict Talley or Hinton on murder charges due to lack of evidence to proceed to trial. Hinton was set free just as his wife believed he would be.

As I look back years later with fresh eyes on the Columbus, Mississippi case, I truly believe there was a serial killer or two killers working as team. If you examine the five murders of the elderly, there is a distinct modus operandi in three of the victims. Louise Randall was gagged, bound, and strangled in an organized crime scene and so was Betty Everett. Robert Hannah was also found gagged, bound, and strangled; but the crime scene was contaminated by a fire. The murders were all about the money. The five murders in Columbus, Mississippi grow colder every year. As long as the murders are not solved, the cases cannot be closed. But the likelihood of a conviction fades, and the community carries a deep scar that cannot heal.

CHAPTER 8

Atlantic City: Eastbound Strangler

On November 20, 2006, four women were found in a drainage ditch just behind the Golden Key Motel along the Black Horse Pike of Egg Harbor Township in Atlantic City, New Jersey. Barbara Breidor, forty-two years old, had disappeared in October; Molly Dilts, twenty years old, last seen just days before her disappearance; Kim Raffo, thirty-five years old, last seen on November 19; and Tracy Roberts, twenty-three years old, last seen in the hospital that month.

Their bodies were scattered in a line and positioned eastward about sixty feet apart in a ditch that flows into a body of water before spilling into the bay behind the city. The desolate area extending back beyond the casinos was the ideal hunting ground for a serial killer. The victims were clothed but were barefoot. Unfortunately, the water in the ditch had washed away a great deal of the DNA evidence as well as decomposed the bodies. This lack of evidence would obviously make solving the case much more of a challenge. Despite these forensic challenges, Roberts was found to be asphyxiated, and Raffo was found to be strangled with some type of cord or rope. Breidor was able to be identified through dental records. Cocaine, alcohol, and heroin were found in all four of the women's systems.

These four women had worked as prostitutes in the city that had inspired the game of monopoly, the city where salt-water taffy had been conceived. But long before the popular board game was even conceptualized, the Lenni Lenape Native Americans, had lived in Egg Harbor, finding all they needed along Patcong Creek—fish, wild berries, and bird's eggs. It would have been impossible for the first inhabitants to imagine an internationally-known resort city springing up on this coast off the Atlantic Ocean. Even more impossible to imagine was that these four women, young mothers with families, were left behind like debris in what had once been called the "World's Playground."

However, vast changes had occurred since the seven-mile boardwalk had been constructed above the dunes in an effort to keep the posh hotels sand free. A seediness had blighted Atlantic City, and these victims were the tragic evidence of all that had gone wrong.

Atlantic City was an emotional case from the outset. When the four victims were found, a news alert showed a sobering aerial view, and I was immediately carried back to the gut-wrenching crime photos of the Green River Killer. Not only did it bring me back to the horrific killings in the Seattle area, but I instantly understood that we had a man on fire here. Once you grasp the frightening brutality this kind of monster is capable of, there is no mental rest until he is stopped. When Gary Ridgway had begun his twisted spree, he was killing about two prostitutes a week. Clearly, we now had someone moving fast in Atlantic City. These victims had been deposited in that ditch within a month, which meant he was killing every week. These were not the first women he killed, and if he wasn't dead or in jail, they wouldn't be the last.

One of the bleak realities of this case was that the victims were prostitutes. If instead they had been clean *girl-next-door* types, the initial reaction and police-issued rewards would have been far more aggressive. This is not to say that the Atlantic County Prosecutors' Office did not put their best effort into trying to catch the killer. The hardest cases to solve are stranger-on-stranger murders. These were women who were risk takers with strong drug addictions—more than likely the undeniable catalyst that had driven them to the dangerous streets. There was no doubt that Breidor, Dilts, Roberts, and Raffo were merely objects. For the killer, it's only about him and his pleasure, and up close and personal murder is his pleasure.

The sympathy I feel for the victims as well as their families cannot be measured. These women were part of our society. The only difference between them and me is that I was lucky enough to be in recovery and they were not. They were daughters, mothers, and sisters. They should not be looked down upon for being enslaved to drugs. There is no innocent little girl who dreams about growing up to become an enslaved, drug-addicted prostitute. Drug addiction leads to prostitution and leads to women being vulnerable—easy prey.

Questions needed to be answered. Who was he, where was he, and how could we stop him? Since this case was happening in New Jersey, we were receiving calls at STALK immediately from the *Star Ledger* and the *New York Times*. Reporters wanted to gather all they could about the killer. When my team and I first heard the news reports about the murders on November 20, 2006, we were on the case—even before the FBI showed up. My associate, Chief Frank Adams, came up with the moniker for the killer—the "Eastbound Strangler."

Atlantic City was in a state of panic. Of course, the casinos, not wanting any bad press, were extremely concerned. They didn't want tourism to be affected. The powers that be were flexing their political muscles, calling in the FBI, but it seemed the locals didn't want the FBI's involvement because Atlantic City Law Enforcement and the vice detectives felt they knew the streets better than anybody else. Ultimately, the Atlantic County Prosecutor's Office took charge of the investigation, and at that point, there was one colossal mess with which they had to deal. People were scrambling. First responders had trampled all over the crime scene while they were collecting the bodies, destroying any significant DNA, and the end result was a contaminated crime scene. Naturally, everyone was in a frenzy, hustling and rushing to try and catch this killer. It was really a crazy time. The cops were handing out STALK's preliminary profiles to many hotels in the area, as reported by the *New York*

Times Pulitzer Prize-winning reporter, Serge Kovaleski. Serge didn't stop there—he put his heart and soul into investigating this case and checking into people of interest who may have been the killer of these women.

We had worked diligently on the profile of the Eastbound Strangler, and we were hopeful that the case would be solved and the city would find some solace in the resolution. Our profile had numerous updates as time passed:

Atlantic City Serial Killer
(Partial Profile of "The Eastbound Strangler")

This lethal predator is a local male who is very familiar with the Atlantic City area and the disposal site of his victims. He has a very organized personality which influences his personal and everyday activities, including his work. He is very rigid and structured in his everyday life. "A place for everything and everything in its place" would be his motto. He has read (and reads) book on serial killers, and he has some knowledge of crime scenes and crime investigations. He has an extreme foot fetish and has a collection of women's shoes and the shoes of his victims. He has not killed every prostitute he has come in contact with. There are prostitutes who know him for the sexual gratification he gets from their feet. He is nonsocial and likes to keep to himself. He is narcissistic (everything revolves around him), and he is also very concerned with making himself look good in all aspects. He is also extremely opinionated. If criticized or disagreed with, he would become extremely angry or agitated. Although at times, when he wants to, he can be very charming.

In his pre-offense mode, he may have spoken about the sinful nature of prostitution, or he may have voiced economic concerns about prostitutes destroying Atlantic City's value or reputation. In his post-offense mode, he would says things like "They got what they deserved" or "Good riddance." He follows the news of his killings in the media. His hobbies would include art and photography, and his obsessive fantasies would compel him to search for sexually graphic and/or violent pictures in all media. He probably has a prior record of sexual or physical abuse or sexual harassment toward women. He may have recently suffered a setback in his work or in a relationship. This predator is probably detached from his father and was abused as a child. This person has also killed before these recent victims were found, and he will be compelled to continue his murderous ways in the future.

Updated Profile as of 12/4/06 on the Eastbound Strangler

This serial killer indulges himself with alcohol, marijuana, and (at times) cocaine. His female victims are surrogates for his rage against his wife or girlfriend who may now be his ex. He may have lost a lot of money gambling in Atlantic City, which has caused financial problems in his relationships and business. When he encounters a female acquaintance in his everyday life, instead of a normal greeting, his greeting may also include a remark or compliment regarding her shoes. These remarks may be along the lines of "Where did you buy those shoes?" "I would like to tell my wife where to get those shoes." He may even be known for offering women foot massages.

Updated Profile as of 12/11/06
Atlantic City Eastbound Strangler
(The Egomaniac with the Inferiority Complex)

Alfred Adler, MD once said, "Show me a person who believes he is superior, and I'll show you a person who believes he is inferior." This serial killer certainly believes he is superior to others, as shown in his God complex. He believes he is all powerful and that he has the last word over life and death. Whether he is posing his victims to the east for some perverted religious reason or posing them to defame Atlantic City is, of yet, an unanswered question. Another possibility is that this pathological narcissist wants his victims pointed in his direction (toward where he lives) perhaps so he can look across the bay, at a defined landmark, where these women were posed into subservient positions. (Also, perhaps, where he could live out his demented, sex, power, and control fantasies.)

This egomaniac knows he cannot stop his murderous ways. He is not in control of his behavior anymore no matter how much power and control he has exhibited on his victims. He has lost his confidence in himself as a man when it pertains to his relationships or his work. He realizes deep in his heart that he is a failure. His narcissism comes from being love-and-attention deprived in his childhood. An emotional detachment from his father has left him to feel like he is the victim of an overcritical and demeaning mother whose self-destructive prophecy about him he will ultimately fulfill. He tries to kill his self-defeating thoughts and feelings of inferiority through his murderous ways. Unlike his victims, though, he has only succeeded in temporarily burying them alive deep inside his mind. Soon, they will come back to haunt him in the form of mistakes and lead to his demise. He can only escape this tortuous mind-hell by giving himself up to Atlantic City authorities and telling his story to the mass media and the millions of people who are interested in him.

Updated Profile as of 12/25/06
Living to Kill and Killing to Live (You
are always on my mind.)

To understand this serial killer is to look at the analogy between the term obsessive-compulsive behavior and the term addiction. Since we usually relate the term *obsessive* with the serial killer and the term *addiction* with the street prostitute, what actually is the difference?

The answer is *none*! It is just a play on terms and words. As the serial killer is constantly obsessing over his stimulating fantasy of power, control, and sex on a daily basis, he is addicted to this fantasizing which eventually propels him into his hunt for a new victim. This fantasizing can lead to murder. This self-destructive, stimulating process will ultimately lead to his demise. The interesting dynamic to review here is that the crack-addicted prostitute whom he hunts is also addicted to a stimulating experience by using cocaine. That addiction propels her into the world of prostitution to hunt for her finances to support her addiction. This is another self-destructive process which will ultimately lead to her demise. Both use the stimulating process to escape their tortuous, thought-filled reality of low self-esteem, shame, anger, despair, and a hellish depression. As the cocaine-addicted prostitute builds up a tolerance to the drug and needs to increase her dosage to achieve her high, so does the serial killer build up a tolerance to the fantasy and needs to escalate (or enhance) by starting the hunt for a victim to achieve his high.

This addictive process in both has its roots in childhood abuse. Not every woman who has been abused in childhood becomes a drug-addicted prostitute. However, it seems that *all* drug-addicted prostitutes have been abused in childhood. Likewise, not every man who has been abused in childhood will become a serial killer; however, it seems that *all* serial killers have been abused in childhood. In essence, you have two abused people from similar dysfunctional family backgrounds who meet with deadly consequences. This addictive process causes the drug-addicted prostitute to live to use drugs and to use drugs to live. Likewise, again, with this serial killer, his addiction process calls for him to live to kill and to kill to live. Reported child abuse has risen to three times the amount reported in the 1980s. And the vast majority of child abuse historically and presently goes unreported.

Updated Profile as of 2/5/07
Paranoia Will Destroy Ya

This paranoid serial killer is also a *shy guy* who is lacking heterosexual social skills. This lack of such skills results in poor relationships with women. This lack of skills was also caused by severe and early childhood trauma. Since he was traumatized in childhood, some of his daily behavior would be considered extremely childlike and immature by others who know him. He may also have strong religious convictions which propel his rage toward drug-addicted prostitutes.

He is an extremely dangerous man who navigates through his life without feeling guilt. He does, however, feel fear. When the women's bodies were found in Egg Harbor, New Jersey, the news sent a wave of fear throughout his entire body. Presently, he is fearful of being arrested and facing life in prison or the death penalty. He is paranoid for good reason. This man is known and has been seen by others, perhaps while searching for a new disposal site for his next victim. With the fact that law enforcement is getting closer and following up with every tip and lead, he will surely be arrested.

When dealing with a dangerous man like this and trying to stop him from committing his final act of control (which would be suicide, which some serial killers have accomplished), the authorities will probably arrest him while he sleeps to ensure a controlled and safe apprehension.

Updated as of 11/17/15
Reward Offered!

There is a $25,000 one-time grand total reward being offered to person(s) with information that leads to the arrest and conviction of the individual(s) responsible for the murders of these women.

Coming in the next update: "Getting closer!"

Note: If perpetrator is arrested prior to next update, we will obviously not be posting. If you have any information, please call the Atlantic City Police Department at 609-926-4051.

*****

After the release of our criminal profile, we began to receive strange phone calls from a mysterious person, seeming as if the killer could be following STALK's online profile. We decided to play with him by changing parts of the profile in order to cause him stress and sleep deprivation. This was all in an attempt to flush him out and keep him on the run. More than that, we were hoping to scare him into a state of paralysis. We understood that the serial killer has no conscience, but he does, thankfully, have a healthy fear of being caught. We updated our STALK profile several times. We even described how the police were more than likely onto him. And since he was considered so dangerous and to add to our intimidation, we described how he would be arrested late at night when his defenses were down. We felt this would add to his sleep deprivation.

This profile surely was instrumental in pausing this killer in his evil tracks. We had no way of knowing if he was dead or in prison, but we did know that there were no more prostitutes being murdered after our profile came out.

There was no surprise that the media would dive head-first into this tragic news story. *48 Hours Atlantic City, New Jersey, Beyond the Boardwalk* aired on May 19, 2007. I had never expected to again meet up with Harold Dow, respected CBS investigative reporter, journalist, and correspondent whom I had worked with six years earlier on the *48 Hours* show *Ghosts of Mississippi*. Harold was a stand-up guy and a dogged investigative journalist who was purely interested in getting at the truth and not TV ratings. I was truly honored to have met and worked with him. Dow's program cast new light and interest on this case, something that was much needed since a year had passed and still, there was no suspect in custody.

Dow helped his audience remember who these four women were, to remember the lives that were taken, and those who were left behind with gaping holes in their minds and hearts that could not be healed. He interviewed Breidor's sister, Valerie, who described the way Barbara had always ended sentences with "I love you." She had worked hard at several casinos as a cocktail waitress and had left behind a daughter, Dominique, who had been born in 1997. Barbara was last known to board a bus on October 17, 2006, for Atlantic City. Her sisters were not surprised she was dead because she had been missing for weeks. They spoke of their sister's past, how she had left Penn State after a year, then had a long string of jobs before giving birth to Dominique. Sadly, Barbara was abused by her baby's father, and her heroin abuse followed. Dominique ended up in foster care as her father landed in jail, and Barbara spiraled out of control.

Kim Raffo was known for her sunny disposition. She had two children with Hugh Oslander after marrying in 1989 and moving to Florida. But in 2003, she fell in love with a chef and relocated to New Jersey. They were trying to build a life together, working in the Taj Mahal Casino, but it was a financial struggle; and Kim missed her kids. Crack became their escape, and prostitution was her livelihood. Within three years of moving to Atlantic City, Kim was killed.

Tracy Anne Roberts grew up in a little Delaware town and moved to Atlantic City just one year before her life was extinguished. She was trained as a medical assistant and had her whole future ahead of her. The city was not the right place for Tracy to settle. She became a street girl, working at a strip joint.

Molly Dilts was the most difficult to identify. Her English Bull dog tattoo made her identification possible. Her uncles told *48 Hours*, "She had a lot of good to spread to the world."

Her friend said Molly was shy and quiet and pretty much kept to herself. Molly had escaped the poor Pennsylvania mining town where she was raised and where she had suffered the loss of her mother and brother. Molly left to find a better life. The last contact she had with her family was a phone call home in October. She left behind her son, Jeremiah.

"We knew right off the bat this was a serial killer," I gave my sobering opinion to Dow. "He wants to have power and control over the area, over Atlantic City. 'I am Godlike. I have the power over life and death'—he knows he's crossed that point of no return. And yes, he will kill again."

They were women who moved to a new city to create new lives "as people often do in fantasy cities," Dow said.

Police captain, John DeAngelis, told *48 Hours*, "Most likely, there was one killer involved with all four victims…In fact, all four victims were methodically positioned in the same bizarre manner. All were facing east, all with no shoes, no purse, no telephone, no personal belongings. It appears these women were killed just for the sake of being killed."

Dow described how fear had become the prominent note in Atlantic City where the public was trying to come to grips with how these women had ended up dead. I explained to Dow what STALK was trying to accomplish and how a profile should be used as a tool and not be thought of as the be-all and end-all: "The profile's goal is to flush the person out, to try and inform the public, and to help stimulate the investigation." I went on to describe the killer. "He's very comfortable with this area. He's local. He's from the area."

Providing more in-depth detail, I explained how the killer could be artistic, pursuing photography or the visual arts. "Watching many of these serial killers, what we see is this underlying artistic nature. John Wayne Gacy was into painting. Henry Lee Lucas was constantly painting." I wrapped up my assessment by saying the killer would be "very shy, more to himself. He's a loner and a patron of prostitutes. The stroll areas are his hunting grounds, and drug-addicted prostitutes are his prey—a man on a mission, and his mission is to eliminate prostitutes."

He was sending some sort of demented message by positioning his victims eastward. Perhaps this was a sign of reference to the holy lands of Jerusalem or Mecca.

In 2009, prosecutor Ted Housel assigned additional investigators to the case as well as relying on both state and federal resources as a task force. They were combing through data from coast to coast. Although they questioned several suspects, no arrest had been made. Three suspects had been questioned and released. Then a handyman, Terry Oleson, a thirty-five-year-old from New Jersey, was suddenly questioned.

Oleson worked at the Golden Key Motel in front of the ditch where the victims were found. He was a loner who fit a number of the characteristics of our profile. His house was raided, and they discovered that he had videotaped a girl of fourteen, his girlfriend's daughter, in various states of undressing. Voyeurism can be a risk factor for a sexual predator. Oleson also had cameras and fences around his house—another red flag. Most serial killers have a good amount of paranoia woven into their personalities. Still to me and the rest of the STALK team, he was just another person of interest. In the beginning, Oleson cooperated with the police, even providing a DNA sample. The Prosecutor's Office did not identify him as a suspect nor was he dismissed.

A year later in 2010, the ex-husband of Kim Raffo, Hugh Auslander, spoke to the media regarding his lack of faith in the case ever being solved. Auslander was disheartened that it had been over a year since he had been contacted by the police, so he had begun his own digging, examining similar cases across the country to no avail.

When ten bodies were found on Gilgo Beach, Long Island, authorities considered a correlation between New York and New Jersey, but to me, this seemed unlikely. Six of the victims were ultimately identified as prostitutes. Despite this coincidence, serial killers all have a distinct signature. There were too many disparities between these two cases. The Atlantic City killer had picked up his victims from the streets in his vehicle whereas the Long Island killer had utilized Craigslist or other online sites. It was also clear that the Long Island killer had not wanted his victims' bodies to be discovered whereas the Eastbound Strangler had posed his victims on the bank of the drainage ditch as if he needed to display them. The only apparent common denominator was that one of the Atlantic City victims had spent a little over a month on Long Island with her husband just before her murder.

Not surprising, the publicity of the Atlantic City case did not end with *48 Hours*. In February of 2012, *Dark Minds* aired on Investigation Discovery the Atlantic City episode on the East Bound Strangler. We covered the large scope of the case, the task force that had devoted over two hundred hours on the murders, both FBI and federal and state forensic authorities all investigating, and yet still no suspect was in custody six years later. "If you take a look at the structure, he has the girls approximately sixty feet apart. One, two, three, four...this is a very structured individual," I concluded on the show. "If he's leaving them out, he's leaving them out to say something. He wants to come back and look at them."

As usual, I consulted 13 regarding this unsolved case. We could only speak for fifteen minutes at a time, so our conversation had to be focused. I found our interactions to be intense; I had no idea of what 13 would say. This is an incarcerated serial killer with no degree in criminology. He's not a psychologist, and he's not a homicide detective. His impressions on this case will only be based on what he can draw from his own personal evil horrific experiences.

"The Atlantic City killer," I said to 13.

"You know this happened during I believe it was the Democratic Convention in Atlantic City...that had to bring every hooker out from the deepest dark alleys when a convention is in town," 13 responded. I personally felt there was no convention at that time.

"Can you tell me why this guy in Atlantic City strangled them, and he didn't stab them, shoot them, hit them over the head? Why strangle?" I asked.

"Let me see…when you strangle somebody that's close and personal, you can feel the life just flow out of the body. Also, he could strangle them because he knows he has to move the bodies and he doesn't want any blood in his car. I think he wanted to see his victims suffer, and I think he did that very well. That's it."

We had a second session with 13. One thing was abundantly clear—in talking to this depraved criminal, I learned dark things about the psychopathic criminal mind that I could not have learned in any classes or from any books. Our dark conversations gave me a better understanding of the predator being hunted. I understood 13's rules were constructed, so he could keep his power and his control. If I wanted his perspective, then we had to play his game. I needed to maintain my intellect over my emotion. This relationship was essential—all the information he could provide was key, and I couldn't allow emotion to destroy this carefully-tended relationship.

13 said, "There was a cluster site of four women, their shoes were gone. This guy had a foot fetish." 13 was in agreement that the shoes are trophies and the killer has a foot fetish. There is a definite sexual component. It was all too clear that

13 understood the East Bound Strangler's mind. I agreed with him.

"A lot of these guys are into strangling because that is the ultimate power and control in a way because you can actually play God. They strangle them until they go out of consciousness, then they bring them back to consciousness, and then they strangle them out again. They keep reliving it over and over until finally they do kill them," I explained on the show.

Tim Braun, a retired homicide detective and cold-case veteran, has worked on over five hundred murders. Braun and his partner, Danny Baldwin, caught nurse Charles Cullen, the most prolific serial killer in New Jersey known as the "Angel of Death."

Braun's keen insight was needed to solve the Atlantic City murders. Braun offered his thoughts on *Dark Minds*. "In my opinion, it's an individual who's local to the area, and I believe he returned on several occasions—not just to dispose of the bodies but also to revisit in some sick way—his work, revisit his work. There was a fantasy, basically reliving the fantasy when he revisits his victims. He may have kept the victim's footwear as a bit of a trophy, another way to revisit his crime without actually going to the scene."

We interviewed clinical psychologist Ed Merski as well for this *Dark Minds* segment. Merski is an expert in abnormal sexuality who practices in New Jersey. He explained that those who have a foot fetish are typically male, and the foot obsession usually has its roots early on, often in adolescence. For people with foot fetishes, normal everyday encounters don't provide what they desire. This fetish, however, is sexually powerful—a wholly stimulating experience.

For a serial killer with a foot fetish, Merski said, "They'll take these items and either rub them on their face or their hands, or they smell them, or they touch them somehow. So even when they're not committing a murder, they're in between. They've got the fantasies going…"

In my final fifteen-minute conversation with 13 regarding the Atlantic City case, he said, "I think he's not in Atlantic City anymore."

Unfortunately, the investigation had stalled after two main people of interest had not panned out. I understood that serial killers kill to live and live to kill. This man could not stop; he was addicted to power and control and taking a woman's life just like 13. I said to 13, "All serial killers are addicts, and they won't stop until they're caught."

"Somebody who can kill that many women and not leave a clue has to be pretty smart or lucky," 13 responded.

"Why do you think he stopped killing?" I asked.

"I don't think he did. I think he's not in Atlantic City anymore. Now this case is very similar to the one on Long Island."

13 was referring to ten victims found in 2010–2011, one 130 miles from Atlantic City. Police had come to believe that at least four of the victims were murdered by a serial killer, but the verdict was still out on whether or not the cases in New Jersey and New York were connected.

"This almost mirrors the Atlantic City case," 13 said. "This guy has a boat. He invites a young lady out on his boat where I'm telling ya nobody can hear her scream. That's it." One more chilling and illuminating conversation with a convicted serial killer had come to an end.

Here we are, more than a decade away from the senseless murders of four New Jersey women. This sort of brutal and unsolved case carries a tragically sad tone. There is somebody out there who knows something, and that means the case is still solvable. We had hoped and prayed that by the tenth anniversary, these killings would be solved. But there was still no closure in 2015 with the people of interest. Oleson, who had served only a short amount of time for privacy violation, and the "River Man" who had been brought to the attention of the police by a sex worker and other people of interest were not leading to any arrest. So STALK offered a $25,000 reward for information leading to the arrest and conviction for the murder of any of the four women. Basically, we set up an incentive for anyone with information to come forward. We all know that rewards work, money talks, and there had simply been too many dead-ends. We felt a suspect for one murder would be instrumental in catching the killer of all the women whose lives had been extinguished.

The Golden Key Motel was demolished in the summer of 2015. In the half century since it had been built, seediness and stigma had come to define the twenty-dollar-a-night motel. Though the motel has been gone for several years and revitalization of the area is the goal, the unsolved murders of four women will continue to linger in the seaside air.

Remember their names: Barbara Breider, Kimberly Raffo, Tracy Ann Roberts, and Molly Jean Bilts.

CHAPTER 9

Molly Bish

O n a calm summer day, June 27, 2000, Molly Bish, a six-
teen-year-old girl was abducted from Comins Pond in
Warren, Massachusetts. Maggie Bish, her mother, dropped her
off at work, and their last words were a goodbye and a love you
before the day's responsibilities were to begin—an exchange so
familiar to us all. The lot was empty as Maggie Bish drove off
just before ten in the morning. The local kids, not yet having
arrived to wade into the pond with Molly to watch over them,
perched atop her life guard chair.

Molly was a responsible daughter, an honor-roll student,
and an athlete. And this was only the beginning of her second
week as a life guard at the pond. A conscientious and beautiful
girl like Molly was a likely and easy target for a predator. From
what the scene at Comins Pond provided, someone had surely
asked Molly for assistance. She had opened the first aid kit and
must have rushed off in a hurry as her shoes and purse were left
behind. At the time of Molly's disappearance, there were quite

a number of sex offenders in the area of Warren; in addition, the police also questioned her boyfriend and her boss but found no leads.

The Bish's had moved their family from Detroit to this charming New England community to provide their three children with a safe upbringing. You wouldn't have anything else in mind but a peaceful life in the twenty-eight-mile town the Bish family choose, graced by woods and a river that meanders through its center. You wouldn't think twice about dropping your daughter off at Comins Pond. This was back when the world seemed less off-kilter. There is no denying that the universe has a way of puzzling us all, and there is a cruel irony that Molly Bish had the impetus as a ten-year-old girl to write these words to console the parents of Holly Piirainen who had been abducted at the age of ten in 1993 less than ten miles from the Bish home:

"I am very sorry. I wish I could make it up to you. Holly is a very pretty girl. She is almost as tall as me. I wish I knew Holly. I hope they found her."

The reason STALK became involved in the Molly Bish case in 2000 was due to one of our team members, Ruth Moore, a nurse specialist who was concerned about a number of murders taking place in various towns of Massachusetts beginning with the letter *W*.

Ruth herself had nearly been abducted as a child in the very same state. She was grabbed and nearly pulled into a car, but she managed to escape. As we examined the Bish case, it struck us as pretty incredible that within a five-or-six-minute window, Molly was whisked away, up a hill which extended behind her lifeguard chair, and then left up another hill, following a path to a graveyard where she must have been loaded into a vehicle before vanishing.

We understood at STALK that the worst torture parents could endure was not knowing what happened to their child or where their child had gone. We put together a preliminary profile for John Bish, Molly's father and his family. Our profile was presented to the media, and we learned years later that Rodney Stanger, a person of interest in her murder, probably read our partial profile in the *Telegram Gazette* newspaper and then jettisoned his family out of town to Florida. These are the things you come to know after the fact. The things that you think about in the middle of the night.

While working on this case, I came into contact with Tim McGuigan and his partner, state policeman Robert Benoit. Tim was a cop working for North Brookfield police department who knew the area, the streets, and their inhabitants very well. Trooper Benoit was older and much more experienced and refined with many more years on the job. He too was well acquainted with the area and the whole state for that matter. Both had been involved with the Holly Piirainen case seven years prior. When we first met, McGuigan had three young daughters; and he was struggling, kind of going-over-the-edge emotionally with the disappearance of Molly Bish.

McGuigan and I spoke constantly about this case, and it was plain to see he was completely obsessed with it. He was a dogged cop and investigator, and I was proud to work with him. Unfortunately, he ended up quitting or was fired from the police force. I'm not clear exactly what transpired, but the end result was we were asked to consider excluding McGuigan from the Bish case. Despite his personal and career glitches, I recognized McGuigan's devotion to these two unsolved cases, and I continued to work with him. "What's bigger in life than getting a predator off the streets before he grabs somebody else?" he had questioned.

Well, as fate would have it, McGuigan ended up going to a bar one night and having a discussion with a woman about Molly Bish and Holly Piirainen and the book he was attempting to write. I had recommended to McGuigan that he journal for therapeutic reasons to get some of the traumatic thoughts out of his mind and onto paper. During his conversation with this woman, he gave some details about the Molly Bish case. And once again, the universe and God offered up an undeniably eerie and spiritual coincidence. This woman's brother, Rick Beaudreau, had been hunting in the woods of Warren when he came across a blue bathing suit on Whiskey Hill. Molly Bish had been wearing a blue Nike bathing suit the day she disappeared. Now you have to understand that it was just by luck this guy spotted this article of clothing, and it struck him as odd because how many bathing suits are found out in the middle of nowhere in the woods?

So he and McGuigan went back out together to search for the bathing suit and found it; at that point, McGuigan called his partner, Trooper Benoit, and me. Then I called my partner Frank Adamson who agreed that was a place where a bathing suit shouldn't be. However, there was no evidence of her remains. The suit was tested for Molly's DNA, and there was a match. So they conducted a search, the biggest investigative search in Massachusetts. They combed those woods meticulously, and they found twenty-six of Molly's bones scattered over a considerable area more than likely due to various predators like coyotes and foxes.

Unbelievable to think that if McGuigan hadn't still been working the case even though he wasn't a cop anymore, if he hadn't spoken about his potential book at the bar that night, he never would have found the hunter. Again, I witnessed how God does work in mysterious ways. So the only way Molly Bish came home, I truly believe this was because of Tim McGuigan. Law enforcement had proposed Molly had possibly run away. There was a possible siting of her down in Florida, but we knew she was not the type of girl to take off, to leave her hand bag, and just vanish. How many females do you know who would take off and leave their purse and other possessions behind? McGuigan was blackballed by the powers that be—even though he outshined them and brought Molly Bish home.

He ended up taking a job as a security guard for about ten dollars an hour and then got his CDL to become a truck driver. Over the years, McGuigan ended up persevering through his trials, tribulations, and torment and moved forward with great success. He now owns his own company and truck, hauling trailers across the United States. He was an excellent cop, and those of us who were close to the case know who the real hero was here. "I've always felt that they never would have found Molly without Tim," Maggie Bish said herself. "He brought Molly home…"

Sadly to date, there have been no arrests made in the Molly Bish case. Rodney Stanger, who was a resident of Southbridge, Massachusetts, for over twenty years, and took off for Florida after our profile was released by the media, is sitting in prison for the murder of his girlfriend, Crystal Morrison. Stanger fits the composite drawing done from Maggie Bish's recollection of a heavyset man with a moustache she had seen sitting in a white car in the parking lot of Comins Pond the day before her daughter was abducted. She had waited protectively in her car until he drove away.

Another witness placed a car resembling the Stanger's at the cemetery which was connected to the pond by a footpath. After the Stanger's moved to Florida, no further abductions happened in the area. Their white car mysteriously disappeared and was never found. Coincidentally, Stanger had grown up in the area and hunted in the woods where Molly Bish's remains were recovered in 2003. The police questioned Stanger about Molly Bish and Holly Piirainen. Two composite sketches of a man between the ages of forty-five and fifty-five with dark salt-and-pepper hair were released.

Twelve years after Molly Bish disappeared, Bonnie Kiernan was retrieving her deceased sister's belongings from Stanger's trailer home when she came across some suspicious items.

"There were an awful lot of hair ties, scrunchies, and barrettes that wouldn't fit my sister's age," Kiernan told CBS Boston. Some of the things that have been learned about Stanger have been concerning. Often, killers keep trophies or items removed from their victims to remind them of their crimes. Stanger exhibits risk factors for being a serial killer. There is no way to say categorically whether Stanger has killed anyone aside from his girlfriend, but I would bet that the murder of Morrison was not his first kill. I would also bet that the items her sister found could be trophies to relive his experiences with other possible victims.

Kiernan was quoted in the media as saying that her sister had given hints in a telephone call that Stanger had been involved in two unsolved killings in Massachusetts—as well as having killed Molly Bish. Stanger, one of our persons of interest, fits our STALK profile to a *T*. His brothers are scary people as well—from what we were able to gather from various victims who had never wanted to come forward and press charges, as is so often the case.

What STALK uncovered in our investigation was a whole family who followed Stanger—the oldest brother, a complete psychopath and a terrifically evil person. But as with so many other frustrating cold cases, the years pile on and the evidence fades. We and everyone else are praying that some new DNA techniques can answer the question—who killed Molly?

Thomas P. Shamshak, a renowned private investigator, worked tirelessly and hard on the case for no money. Shamshak was a close friend to the Bish family as well as being one of the first investigators to identify definite red flags with Stanger. He confirmed Stanger's fondness for hunting and fishing at Comins Pond and the surrounding area where Molly Bish's remains were discovered. Stanger's violent propensities were also confirmed, his physical abuse to his wife and baby, as well as any unfortunate animals he tired of along the way.

In an article published on February 8, 2009 in the *Republican Newsroom*, Nancy H. Gonter wrote:

> Shamshak said he was struck by the similarities between Rodney Stanger and the profile of Bish's abductor done years ago by John Kelly of the Old Bridge, N.J.-based STALK Inc. For example, Kelly's profile notes that the abductor would have employment that centers around his "visual intake sense" such as tree-trimming, computers, car repair or cleaning.
>
> "He is very familiar with Comins Pond, and probably has fished there," the profile states.

The profile states the abductor would have a history of physical or sexual assaults on females, would be a white male, and his drugs of choice would be nicotine, alcohol, cocaine and marijuana. His hobbies would include hunting, fishing, photography or gambling.

When Stanger's ex-wife had first met Rodney, he was employed at a factory in Sturbridge where Holly Piirainen had lived, and following this job, he went to work for a tree service until he claimed a back injury and went on disability.

Working with STALK to piece together these profiles is a somber task but one that is absolutely necessary. Our hopes are to prevent other innocent lives from being lost and to provide the families of victims with answers and, hopefully, an arrest. When I am working on a case, I can't help but flashback to my early days. Words and images flood back to me from a chapter experienced so long ago by such a different version of myself that it hardly seems possible. I remember being told, "If you learn how to kill smaller things, then you can work your way up to bigger things…like people." This came from a hard psychopath coming out of prison. I can remember hearing someone on the street bragging that he'd "just laid him out" or "yeah, I just gave him a new face!" or "Don't get mad. Get even!"

My education on the street has afforded me an insight that most would want to refuse. I have an edge because of the world I was immersed in when I was young; I was weaned by psychopaths. I know how they think and act, and I survived by learning how to read them fast. There is a comfort in believing I have taken my past and turned it into a tool for good. Thanks God!

Molly Bish was laid to rest on August 2, 2003, on what would have been her twentieth birthday. The unsolved murders of two girls with promising futures ahead linger in the air of Massachusetts, and two families continue to be left flailing in the dark, grieving with no answers.

CHAPTER 10

The Woodsman

Between 2003 and 2007, five young women's skeletal remains and one severely decomposed body were discovered in the woods of Massachusetts. Ironically, Worcester, where three of the victims were from, is known as the "heart of the Commonwealth" due to its central location in the state. The city of nearly forty square miles was built upon an underground river and eleven hills.

There were many high-profile cases, mostly in the northeast, that we had been able to help out with. And the Woodsman case was one of the biggest. The media covered the tragic murders for years. Google "Woodsman" or "Main South Woodsman," and you will find countless articles and newscasts spanning years. These female victims were all young, dark-haired, dark-skinned, and petite; they were all mothers and, sadly, had been mixed up with drugs and prostitution in the south area of Worcester.

The first victims found were Betzaida Montalvo and Carmen Rudy in September 2003. Both women were twenty-nine years old and had the horrible misfortune of crossing paths with the same monster. Montalvo and Rudy were discovered in shallow graves in the woods near a Marlboro private school, Hillside, eighteen miles from Worcester and convenient to the highway. Montalvo, the mother of five, was last seen in April of 2003. When she was found, she was in her pajamas and was still wearing her silver-heart bracelet which read, "Number one mom." Her body was discovered by students from the private school.

Rudy was found only a hundred yards away from Montalvo and less than a week later. She had been missing nearly a year and left two children behind. Both victims' bodies were approximately two hundred yards from the road. Jackie Rudy, the older sister of Carmen, spoke to *Dark Minds* for a 2012 episode "The Woodsman."

"She came to my house, and she borrowed an outfit to wear for a job interview she had the next day. She was really trying to get her life together. She wanted to get her kids back. She wanted to have a happier family. But she never came back.

"And I knew then that she never was going to come back. And I know that she was really, really trying to get her life back on track...and she did it. She came to my house every single day, and she was staying clean. And for her just not to come back that one day...I knew there was something wrong."

Within a year, Dinelia Torres's body was found in the woods just a few yards off a gated road in Hudson by a utility worker—not far from where Montalvo and Rudy were discovered. Torres was only thirty-three and had gone missing in August of 2003. She also, like the other two victims, was involved with prostitution. Unfortunately for all three, decomposition obscured cause of death and prevented the gathering of DNA evidence. This means the three cases could neither be linked together nor tied to a specific suspect.

Tragically, the victims did not end here. Wendy Morella, who was the mother of two and only forty years old, was last seen on September 1, 2004, when she left home. If this was the same killer, he broke his pattern. Morella was found by a man out for a walk twelve days later in York, Maine, one hundred and fifty miles away from Worcester, in a garbage can.

I believed *staging* was at play here. Staging is the act of trying to throw off the cops. This killer had left so many bodies around Worcester. He probably attempted to throw a wrench into the investigation by staging a body in a trash can in Maine—away from Massachusetts's jurisdiction. This was what Gary Ridgway, the Green River Killer, had done by taking a body part of one of his victims to Oregon.

The frightening reality is that these evil monsters are among us. They come across as very charming, very nice, and very willing to help—they are liked by those who know them. This is the kind of guy you're dealing with—a master manipulator. Think of Ted Bundy, so smooth that Carole Ann Boone married him while he was on death row.

At this point, although I could ascertain many similarities to Gary Ridgeway, this serial killer was, without a doubt, more refined in his choice of victim.

It was in 2007 when thirty-five-year-old Lineida Olivera's skeletal remains were found near Rutland State Forest, two hundred yards off Route 122, by a hunter. According to local reporter, Scott Croteau, who had followed this story from the beginning: "Authorities had a suspicion a serial killer might be at work considering the women were all prostitutes, petite, and Hispanic-looking." It seemed all were drug addicted or too clear that Olivera fit both the occupational and physical description that would link her to the Woodsman. Scott Croteau, was a dogged reporter who cared deeply for the Woodsman's victims and the suffering they endured. He also interviewed their families and was up close and personal to see the agony they were going through. Scott, Worked this case from beginning to end thoroughly. I believe he put a lot of pressure through his many articles on the Woodsman, which probably slowed him down, and reduced his number of victims. That's what we at STALK INC hoped for. Flush him out and keep him running in fear! It was our honor and pleasure to work with Scott.

Our five-person team worked hard at STALK to compile a profile which we made public in 2007—though we still considered it a work-in-progress. This was our way of keeping the murders of all these women from being forgotten. The multi-agency task force created to catch the Green River Killer years prior was the logical way to proceed with the Woodsman case. The task force included detectives and investigators on four levels—local, county, state, and federal.

Frank Adamson, vice president of STALK and former chief of criminal investigations in Seattle's King County sheriff's office, understood the value of pumping substantial resources into horrific cases like these—when so many are tragically affected. Clearly, this killer was the ultimate hunter and predator who had the intelligence and the skill not to be caught.

It was obvious that the Woodsman targeted a particular type, and he was very wisely choosing women he determined would not be missed. Our profile was made available online—a male no younger than twenty-eight years old, working in the construction field, and a truck driver or maintenance worker. He would enjoy fishing, hunting, and viewing pornography. He may have a criminal history of breaking and entering, DWI, and drug possession, possibly dealing, as well as a history of assaulting women, cruelty to animals, trespassing, and being a Peeping Tom.

The Woodsman would have a learning disability and suffer from anxiety and paranoia after being raised in a physically-and-sexually-abusive home for which he would blame his mother. He would be a heavy smoker who abuses alcohol, marijuana, and, occasionally, cocaine. He would be a frequent user of prostitutes who may know him to prefer sex outdoors, and he would be known to the prostitutes of the Main South area of

Worcester. He would also be a compulsive bragger who talks of his fishing and hunting exploits and conquests. He would drive a pickup truck or large sport utility vehicle. The following is the actual STALK profile as it appeared online:

The Power Is in the Questions
February 4, 2008

A question that begs to be answered is where the Woodsman get the white prep cook's shirt, which he gave to Windy Morello. How did he have access to such a shirt? Did he work in a place where such shirts were required? Did he transport such shirts for one reason or another? Or does he have access to a place where such shirts may be stored? The prostitutes working the Main South district of Worcester may be able to relate a John to one or more of these questions.

Evolving Profile on the Main South Woodsman Effective
September 17, 2007

We are expanding previous information pertaining to the age of the Woodsman. We profiled the age of the Woodsman between twenty-eight to forty-one years old. However, we now believe that the age of the Woodsman could be older than forty-one years but still not younger than age twenty-eight. May God bless Wendy Morello.

Wendy Morello's murder seems to reveal the most information to help identify the Woodsman. Wendy was last seen at her friend's residence in Worcester, Massachusetts, between 4:00 and 5:00 a.m. on September 5, 2004. She was said to have run out of the room to get into a vehicle with someone and supposedly was not dressed up to work the street at that time.

Instead, she was wearing jeans, sneakers, and a black shirt. We believe she knew the person in the vehicle and felt safe with him. She was never seen again, and her body was found on September 13, 2004, on Riverwood Drive in York, Maine. When she was found, she was in a plastic garbage can, wearing a white shirt (not the black one she left the house with). This suggests to us that Ms. Morello stayed with this person for some length of time before he killed her. She knew him. She felt safe with him, and she stayed with him. *Where* did she stay with him is the question!

Is there a person who owns or rents a building or house where prostitutes from Main South in Worcester feel safe going to in order to get high or turn tricks for money or drugs? We believe the girls from Main South probably have the answer to that question.

Worcester, MA Serial Killer
(Profile of the "Main South Woodsman")

Gender: Male (local to area)

Race: Unknown at this time

Age: Between the ages of twenty-eight to forty-one with a visual primary intake sense.

Vocations: Works in the construction field or is (or has been) a truck driver or maintenance worker.

Hobbies: Fishing, hunting, pornography (in all forms of media)

Legal History: A history of assaulting women, and he probably assaulted some prostitutes who got away from him. He would have charges of breaking and entering, a history of DUIs, or possession of an illegal substance. He may have even been known as a drug dealer. He has a history (although maybe not legal history) of cruelty to animals, trespassing, and being a Peeping Tom.

Mental History: This psychopath suffers from a learning disability and suffers from anxiety and paranoia.

Drug and Alcohol History: This perpetrator is a heavy smoker who abuses alcohol, marijuana, and, at times, cocaine. He probably has received some treatment for alcohol and/or substance abuse.

Psycho-Social History: Grew up in a very physically and sexually abusive household as a child and blames his mother for the abusive situation. He is addicted to frequenting areas of prostitution, and he is known to prostitutes in the Main South area of Worcester. He may be known to prostitutes as being a john who prefers sex outdoors, weather permitting. He is a compulsive bragger who brags about his fishing and hunting exploits. He would brag about and enjoy showing pictures of his fishing and hunting conquests.

Vehicle: Drives a pick-up truck or a large SUV.

We will be reporting much more about this particular predator in the following weeks. He should turn himself into the authorities to end his personal torturous torment and his addiction to killing. He can then tell his story to the millions of people who are interested in him.

******

After we released our profile, there was a flurry of publicity. Scott Croteau wrote a thorough article in the *Telegram and Gazette* that encapsulated our profile and discussed the team of STALK, Chief of Detectives Frank Adamson who had come on board after retiring from the King County sheriff's department the Seattle area; Dr. Edward Merski, head psychologist; John Lewkowicz, a sex addiction specialist; Ruth Moore, a psychiatric nurse specialist; and myself. Croteau wrote:

> Mr. Kelly said the profile was released because his organization wants the killings to end and the man responsible brought to justice. He said people have to appreciate that the slain women are people even if they were prostitutes and battled drug addiction.
>
> The physical similarities led the profilers to choose the potential professions listed in the profile. Construction workers and maintenance workers are visually hands-on people, Mr. Kelly said, adding that truck drivers have a *good eye*.

The article quoted me as saying, "Not every male that is abused as a child becomes a serial killer, but it seems every serial killer has been abused either physically or sexually." This sad truth is not meant to be any type of excuse but is meant to illuminate for better understanding. I further explained, "The killer is also picking women as his victims because he believes he is killing his mother." This psychological component is key to putting the twisted pieces of the serial killer puzzle together as well. There are many ways for sick individuals to feel powerful—drug dealing and killing are obvious methods.

From all my in-depth work with addiction and, in particular, with the addiction of serial killing, it had become painfully clear that these killers don't feel guilt or remorse. What they do feel is extreme fear and terror when a body is found. This individual would be plagued by haunting questions, like whether or not he had been seen with the victim, whether or not his vehicle was spotted or his license plate number was captured, or whether or not he had left any evidence behind—like a strand of his hair.

The STALK profile was done pro bono, and once it was posted online, any law enforcement officials had access to our carefully considered assessment.

When I spoke to 13 about this case, he had quite a lot to say, and there was no doubt in my mind that these two killers had a frightening amount in common. I asked 13 during our conversation on *Dark Minds* if he believed the Woodsman killed his victims outdoors.

"Outdoor crime scene. Definitely. They go off to a secluded location to do what they do. Motel screams can easily be heard…not to mention all the fingerprints and DNA that can be left behind. I think the Woodsman is smarter than that."

Some serial killers choose the outdoors because the elements make the crime scene more challenging to find conclusive evidence. The longer the body remains outside, the harder it is on the investigators.

"Why drug-addicted prostitutes?" I asked 13.

"They're easy. You know, you throw a twenty-dollar bill at her or a fifty, and they'll go anywhere with ya."

In a further conversation with 13, I asked if he believed the Woodsman would be an outdoorsy-type guy—someone fond of hunting and fishing.

"Yes, definitely."

"Okay, what kind of a job do you think this guy had?"

"What would give somebody time off from work? Well, if the guy was a roofer, I don't think steel workers or masons work on rainy days. Dry-wall guys can't work or electricians. You got a lot of guys sitting in a gin mill, you know, depressed."

"And the booze would uninhibit him…right?"

"Oh, that would encourage. You know this is just what everybody would think is just an everyday guy. Now only the people really, really close to him may know that he may have a dark side."

13 offered us another theory: "I think these girls are all surrogates for somebody he has a lot of anger against."

I needed 13 to elaborate: "Talk about that anger that he has in himself."

"There's this dominant woman in his life."

"And she hurt him in some way?" I urged.

"She hurts him, belittles him. He just resents that so much. Of course, you know he probably hates himself too for allowing this to happen."

13 was more than likely hitting upon something all too relevant. It's a basic human tendency to rely upon our mothers for care and protection, but when our needs are not met in our early years or we grow up in a dysfunctional family, often, anger is the end result. When that anger becomes internalized, it can erupt. The Woodsman could very well be punishing his victims for the abuse and neglect he suffered all those years when he was most in need and most vulnerable. Not likely a coincidence that all of the victims were mothers themselves.

When you read about murders in the papers, see a quick spot on the nightly news. There is never enough time afforded to the victims, to the victims' families, to the utter devastation that is left in the wake of a brutal killer. The emphasis is on finding the psychopath who is leaving dead bodies strewn in desolate places, and of course, this makes sense. But when you focus on this sort of violent addiction, you cannot ignore. You cannot forget the pain and suffering of those who have lost someone they loved—the loss of a parent, the loss of a sibling, the loss of a child, or the loss of a friend.

During the filming of *Dark Minds,* Evelyn Rudy, the mother of Carmen Rudy, spoke vividly about who her daughter was before her life was taken. "She was beautiful. She was smart. Loved animals…she loved everybody…really. She had her children taken away from her because she was on drugs. We tried everything we could to straighten her out, but she just wasn't ready yet.

"She was just about ready to get her children back. The day she went missing, she went out for a job interview. And she was very happy about that. She really did want to work and straighten her life out. My daughter, Jackie, reported her missing. For a whole year, we were looking for her. Everybody who passed us on the street looked like her, and it was terrible."

Unfortunately, as I stated on *Dark Minds,* "You can't convict on coincidence." And at that point in time, all law enforcement could do was eliminate suspects and move on to the next person of interest.

On June 2, 2008, journalist Nancy Cicco@Seacoastline. com, wrote an article "Profile of a Serial Killer: Maine Murder May Play a Role in Investigation." Miss Cicco wrote of forensic evidence that could help solve the series of brutal murders that had plagued the northeast:

> John Kelly, president of System to Apprehend Lethal Killers of New Jersey, says the background of Alex F. Scesny, named as a "person of interest" in the case by Massachusetts

authorities, in some ways fits the profile his group compiled of the type of person who could have committed the crimes.

Tim Connolly from the Worcester, Massachusetts, district attorney's office, had discussed Scesny as being a possible suspect in Morello's murder. Though she was found in Maine, authorities believed she had not been killed there, and her remains had been there no more than a week.

"Wendy Morello, being found within eight days in a garbage can, is the most recent victim, we believe, of the Woodsman who would present one the of the best chances of trace or DNA evidence because her body was found relatively quickly," the article quoted me stating. "I really think a big key to this case is in Maine."

Finally in the fall of 2008, Alex F. Scesny, a thirty-one-year-old from Berlin, Massachusetts, was charged with raping and murdering Theresa K. Stone of Fitchburg, Massachusetts. Theresa Stone was only thirty-nine years old when she was found partially nude off Kinsman Road in October of 1996; her murder remained a mystery for years.

There were two men who were possible persons of interest: James Webber, who was the father of Stone's child, and who also had a known history of violence; the other suspect was Everett Carlson, a man who was seen often at the same bar Stone frequented. One witness claimed to have seen Stone climb into Carlson's truck just before her murder.

Scesny had been a person of interest in the Main South Woodsman case since he had an alleged history of violence against women as well as a geographic connection to the Marlboro area. Years prior, Scesny listed his residence as 217 Robin Hill Road, Marlboro. This was the property owned by the Hillside School where two of the bodies were found.

Scesny pled not guilty to charges of rape and murder and was held without bail on a September morning in 2008. After a year and a half of prison time due to these assault and battery charges, there was, at last, a stroke of luck. DNA from the rape crime matched the DNA from Theresa Stone.

According to Croteau's May 5, 2008 article in the *Telegram and Gazette,* Scesny's family considered him to be a *peace-keeper.* They, therefore, could not see any way the thirty-eight-year-old construction worker could have played a part in any of the serial murders in Massachusetts that had baffled law enforcement for half a decade.

In March of 2012, Scesny was found guilty of killing Stone although ironically, he was acquitted in the West Boylston rape case. He was sentenced to life without parole. As of 2015, Scesny was not charged with the murders of Olivera, Morello, Rudy, Montalvo, or Torres. Since Scesny's arrest, prostitute murders in Worcester, Massachusetts, have greatly diminished.

Croteau wrapped up Scesny's legal travails in July of 2015 when his murder conviction was upheld by the state's highest court: "While the Supreme Judicial Court found errors with the prosecutor's closing argument in Scesny's trial, the court ruled the jury was not prejudiced because of instructions given to the jury by the judge and the strength of the case against Scesny."

In addition to the many victims from the heart of the Commonwealth, there are eleven murders that have gone cold from 1988 and 1989 in the southeastern region of the state. These women too were petite and were known to be prostitutes with drug issues. Despite the years that have passed, the families of these victims deserve answers.

CHAPTER 11

Through the Lens

When I look back now through all these decades and I see myself as a teenager, a young man, then muscling through my recovery, and finally segueing into my productive career, I can appreciate just how miraculous my journey has been. I was frighteningly delusional in my youth, spending each day just trying to get over—partying, drugs, and gambling, I foolishly believed I was working my way up the ladder. There was a hole inside that I was trying to fill with Cadillacs, power, money, gold, alcohol, and cocaine. I simply never had a sense of self—outside of making money, outside of earning. The truth was, I was doggedly working my way to an early grave. Only by the grace of God did I end up not killing someone or being killed. My life was spent chasing sinful indulgence, and the end result was insanity. I was insane, there's no doubt about it. The irony is that I ended up finding myself, despite my addiction— really, because of my addiction.

When you look at Narcotics Anonymous, they talk about allowing God or your Higher Power to return you to sanity because when people are addicted to drugs, they are insane. Their best thinking is insane thinking, and it has taken them to where they are. They have no clue how it will all end—usually with death or incarceration of some kind. Drug addiction is such a subtle seduction. You start off smoking some pot, drinking some beer, and next thing you know, you're trying something harder. It's all fun. It's all laughs. It's very social. Trouble is that a lot of the people you're socializing with are using harder drugs like coke or heroin, and soon, you're chasing those first highs; and you'll never catch up with it and get it back.

My journey is complicated. But looking back, I can sort through and find a sense of peace and purpose if you have a conscience and you've managed to hold onto your long-term memory, all of the things you've done that were hurtful not just to yourself but to others, stare you in the face.

There's that little boy, six or seven years old, lugging around his Bible, sitting in church each morning, and picturing himself one day all grown-up as a priest. There's also that older boy of thirteen, tossing a football and taking his schoolwork seriously. But then I veered off course at about fifteen, and I found myself wandering onto the streets and into the poolrooms and gambling dens, as all my childhood friends drifted away.

What really interests me is how I managed to escape and how I managed to survive and accomplish all that I did. So many of my old-street family are gone now, having plunged into the drug-and-crime culture. No good came from this sort of life. We had a saying, "If you go slow, you gotta go. If you go fast, you can't last."

I have come to believe my survival was a gift from God who has truly run my life and pulled me from the depths of emotional, spiritual, and physical hell. I had poisoned myself with cocaine, overdosed many times, trying to party myself out of this world. I lived through many car accidents where I had been driving under the influence. I had guns pointed at my head, knives held against my throat, and yet I pulled through. I'm here!

And as I sit here today, I am filled with gratitude that he gave me the opportunity to make amends. I mean, it's miraculous that a guy detoxing in 1982 and seeing the Green River Killer in the news could ever imagine that many years later, he would be in the mountains of Washington hunting the worst serial killer in the United States history. That he would transform his life and devote himself to being an addiction counselor, a certified social worker, and to being a criminal profiler. Ten years later, I secured my education, became a senior counselor in a hospital, and then opened my private practice which blossomed into ExtraCare Health Services. Who'd have ever thought I'd be asked in 1995 to be on the Lee Brown Clinton Committee on drug abuse for the eastern United States or defining my addiction theory and publishing *Low Self Esteem, the Beginning of Addiction* in a book and *Warning Signs: A Guidebook for Parents* that helped so many worthy people to heal. All these years later, my theory on low self-esteem, as the foundation of addiction, is coming to the surface. How could I have imagined my tragic prophesy back in 2002, regarding school shootings, would become this frightening reality, or how many children would die? All this tragedy, drug addiction, and senseless killing are rooted in child abuse, low self-esteem, depression and anger.

I attribute my success in helping so many who suffer with crippling addictions to turning myself over to God, to being an instrument of God.

It's all by the grace of God and Christianity is my vehicle. Without God in my life, I would not have known how to live as a decent person. It's true that I turned my back on my God, but obviously, He didn't turn his back on me. My faith was muted by the drugs and by my ego, but once I overcame these daunting obstacles, there was a clear purpose for me, and hopefully I can continue to serve in the years to come. But we all need a direction, and we all need solid teachers. That's why the Stalkinc.com website reads: *You only know what you know from what you learned. Who were your teachers?* Your early teachers shape you, and give you a course to follow, and I had many different teachers. I had teachers who were wise guys and teachers who were from the underworld, and later on, thankfully, I had great highly-educated professionals, professors, and spiritual teachers. The saving grace for me was my Christian foundation, because in the end, when all else failed and everything was lost, where else would I have gone? I went to the church and found the beginning of my miraculous resurrection and salvation. For nearly four decades I have given thanks every single day.

Addiction of any kind, including serial killing, has its roots in negative thoughts. People who feel badly look for something to pull them out of despair. In time I came to understand that I could sell addicts hope, sell them a better life, by selling them on themselves. This idea created the passion in my heart that led me into the addiction field, and my focus was to keep a person's negative image of himself from taking over a session. Criticism although very appropriate does not serve any good purpose, and clearly these were not bad people sitting in my office—they were sick people; they didn't intentionally become addicts, they had not been young children, fantasizing about how they would grow up and become drug-addicted prostitutes, or heroin addicts, alcoholics, or coke addicts. They were hurting and sick individuals who would lose their families and futures and possibly land in jail or die. Addiction is a disease. For me it's all about bringing a positive message to the addict. If he or she wants to recover, that person can recover, but it truly all comes down to self-help. I'll be your guide on the journey down the path, but you have to do the walking.

The beauty is, once they gain confidence they can build on it, and then they feel good from the reward or pleasure center in their brain—from achieving, and from accomplishing those goals, from helping others, from moving forward, from working out, and they can start to stimulate those endorphins in a really smart and natural way without drugs. In addition, if they can turn their issues over to God, and talk to another human being, whether it's a counselor, or somebody in the program, then they are no longer keeping all the pain inside. When that overwhelming stress and pain is turned into language and released—that's when you see miracles take place. Miracles happen. And it's very, very spiritual. You feel there's a higher power working by your side as you help someone to recover. At an older age you see the hardships in your life in a different way; you see the personal spiritual growth, and all of your potential because of what you've overcome. There is an understanding of all the good you can do in the world and you grasp the bigger design.

There is a phrase that seems ironic—*grateful addict*—defined as people who've been in recovery for a good period of time who can look back on all the heartache they've experienced, all the pain that they put their families through, and they can make amends when possible. There is genuine reason to feel grateful.

You know, I look at it all now as a very sad but positive experience. Certainly something I couldn't even begin to entertain thirty-some years ago. If I had not gone through all those years of hardship, I would not be who I am today, and because of who I am today, thousands of families and addicts have gotten better in the course of my three decades in the field. I'm just so honored to have had the privilege of serving them. I feel so elated and humble that I was able, with my great team of counselors at ExtraCare, to help each of them. Although we couldn't cure them, we were guides on their journey. And thankfully, we could relate to (pretty much everyone) who needed help and counseling.

In the years to come, my major focus will be to continue helping families deal with addiction as well as the underlying dynamics that cause addiction. That's where I'll still be putting my full effort.

The most important thing to realize is if I could accomplish what I've accomplished, others can too. I accomplished my recovery and fulfilling career through spirituality and turning my life over to Jesus. Jesus is my Lord and God, and God is my Master and Creator; and this faith has worked for me. I told Marilyn, "When I die and you bury me, the best thing to put on my gravestone is 'God is the answer.'"

And she said, "Yeah, but what's the question?"

I replied, "Listen, bottom line: God is the answer to all questions."

About the Author

John Kelly

John Kelly is a born again Christian and a renowned criminal profiler, psychotherapist, and addiction specialist. In his 1992 paper "The Alcohol, Drug, and Serial Killer Connection," he was the first theorist to label serial killing as an addiction. Kelly's profiling expertise was used in (over 100 cases), including well-known cases such as the Green River Killer, the Molly Bish case, and the Atlantic City Murders.

Kelly's efforts as a profiler have led to three appearances on CBS's *48 Hours* and multiple interviews on CNN Primetime with Nancy Grace, FOX—Geraldo at Large, New Jersey Channel 12, and HLN—Jane Velez-Mitchell Show. Also, in the three-season television show *Dark Minds*, Kelly co-hosted and was seen around the world in twenty-two episodes over a three-year span.

John Kelly was also the founder of System to Apprehend Lethal Killers Inc. (STALK) and executive director of ExtraCare Health Services LLC, an outpatient counseling agency for mental health and addictive illness. He is a board certified forensic examiner, a fellow of the American Board of Forensic Examiners, and a national certified addiction specialist. Kelly is also a published author who has written the book *Warning Signs—A Guidebook for Parents.*

John Kelly lives in an undisclosed location with his wife and continues to hunt evil predators.

Jenny Grace

With an MFA in Creative Writing and a career on both sides of the publishing arena—editorial and writing—Jennifer Grace has published many articles in newspapers, magazines and online. She has also published children's books with Simon and Schuster, and short stories with various commercial and literary magazines, as well as in an anthology by Syracuse University Press. She is currently owner of Jenny Grace Editorial and Argyle Ink, and works extensively with clients, literary agents, and on-line publishers in the United States and abroad as an editor, ghostwriter and writing coach. In addition to her MFA, Jennifer continued studies at Sarah Lawrence and Skidmore's Summer Writers Institute with many esteemed writers.

Lightning Source UK Ltd.
Milton Keynes UK
UKHW010737070223
416609UK00002B/354